Picture Books
for Middle and High School? Are You Kidding?

Liz Knowles, Ed.D.

outskirts press

Picture Books for Middle and High School? Are You Kidding?
All Rights Reserved.
Copyright © 2020 Liz Knowles, Ed.D.
v2.0

The opinions expressed in this manuscript are solely the opinions of the author and do not represent the opinions or thoughts of the publisher. The author has represented and warranted full ownership and/or legal right to publish all the materials in this book.

This book may not be reproduced, transmitted, or stored in whole or in part by any means, including graphic, electronic, or mechanical without the express written consent of the publisher except in the case of brief quotations embodied in critical articles and reviews.

Outskirts Press, Inc.
http://www.outskirtspress.com

ISBN: 978-1-9772-2999-1

Cover Photo © 2020 www.gettyimages.com. All rights reserved - used with permission.

Outskirts Press and the "OP" logo are trademarks belonging to Outskirts Press, Inc.

PRINTED IN THE UNITED STATES OF AMERICA

Acknowledgements

Thanks to Dr. Patricia Leland-Jones, longtime friend and Nova doctoral program buddy, for proofreading the manuscript!

Thanks to the faculty at Boca Prep International School, Boca Raton, Florida for the idea!

Thanks to James Tepper, rising 7th grader, for the drawings introducing each subject area. James resides in Jupiter, FL with his family and his two lovable dogs, Magic and Monty. James has always been fascinated with vehicles, especially trains, and architecture of structures in the world around him. That developed into a love of drawing and creating vehicles and architectural styles of his own. James dreams of one day becoming an architect or engineer and owning his own design firm. In the meantime, he enjoys using Minecraft and Legos to bring his creations to life.

A monthly update, with many reviewed, additional titles, will be available to you if you email me at brainfitness78@gmail.com Log on to www.cognitive-fitness.com to see my other work.

Table of Contents

Introduction i

Science 1
    Science 2
    Inventors and Inventions 8
    Astronomers and Astronomy 12
    Architects 13
    Technology 14

Math 17
    Math 18

History 21
    History 22
    David A. Adler – Biographies 30
    Japanese Internment 31
    Holocaust 33
    Slavery 35
    Civil Rights 41
    Immigrants, Refugees, Migrant Workers 47
    Women In History 55
    War 61
    Government 65
    Ancient History 65

Language Arts 71
    Language Arts 72
    Grammar 73
    Cinderella Stories 73
    Creative Writing Ideas 75

The Arts 83
    The Arts 84
    Music 87

Character 91
    Character 92
    Homelessness 97

Miscellaneous 99
    Miscellaneous 100

Liz Knowles, Ed.D. 105

INTRODUCTION

What makes a picture book?

Picture books contain an average of 32 to 40 pages with pictures appearing on every page or every two-page spread.

Picture books for:

- 2 to 5-year-olds have 200 to 400 words
- 3 to 8-year-olds have 500 and 600 words
- 6 to 10-year-old have 1000 to 3000 words

How are exceptional picture books awarded?

The most important picture book award is the Randolph Caldecott that is given annually. Randolph Caldecott (1846-1886) was an English illustrator. The Caldecott Medal "shall be awarded to the artist of the most distinguished American Picture Book for Children published in the United States during the preceding year. The award shall go to the artist, who must be a citizen or resident of the United States, whether or not he be the author of the text."

Here are the last 20 years of Caldecott winners:

2020 Going Down Home with Daddy – Minter
2019 Hello Lighthouse - Blackall
2018 Wolf in the Snow - Cordell
2017 Radiant Child: The Story of Young Artist Jean-Michel Basquiat - Steptoe

2016 Finding Winnie: The True Story of the World's Most Famous Bear - Mattick
2015 The Adventures of Beekle - Santat
2014 Locomotive - Floca
2013 This Is Not My Hat - Klassen
2012 A Ball for Daisy - Raschka
2011 A Sick Day for Amos McGee - Stead
2010 The Lion and the Mouse - Pinkney
2009 The House in the Night - Swanson
2008 The Invention of Hugo Cabret - Selznick
2007 Flotsam - Wiesner
2006 The Hello, Goodbye Window - Juster
2005 Kitten's First Full Moon - Henkes
2004 The Man Who Walked Between the Towers - Gerstein
2003 My Friend Rabbit - Rohmann
2002 The Three Pigs - Wiesner
2001 So You Want to Be President? - St. George
2000 Joseph Had a Little Overcoat - Taback

Other awards often presented to picture books are:

Jane Addams - given annually to a children's book published the preceding year that advances the causes of peace and social equality

Robert F. Sibert - awarded annually to the writer and illustrator of the most distinguished informational book published in English during the preceding year

Orbis Pictus - recognizes books which demonstrate excellence in the "writing of nonfiction for children"

Pura Belpre - presented to a Latino/Latina writer and illustrator whose work best portrays, affirms, and celebrates the Latino cultural experience in an outstanding work of literature for children and youth

Coretta Scott King - given annually to outstanding African American authors and illustrators of books for children and young adults that demonstrate an appreciation of African American culture and universal human values

Charlotte Zolotow Award - awarded for outstanding writing in a picture book published in the United States

Ezra Jack Keats Award - recognizes and encourages authors and illustrators new to the field of children's books

And some of the others:

Horn Book, School Library Journal, American Library Association, New York Times, Junior Library Guild, Bank Street, Kirkus Reviews, etc.

Who creates picture books?

Author/illustrator – same person:

Patricia Palacco
David Wiesner
Anthony Browne
Jane Yolen
Ed Young
Jeanette Winter
Lane Smith Mo Wilems
Henry Cole
Allen Say
Dave Eggers
Peter Sis
Kadir Nelson
Duncan Tonatiuth

Shane Evans
Ruth Heller
Jon Klassen
Peter Reynold
James Ransome
Brian Floca
Alexander Wallner
Emily Arnold McCully
David Macaulay

Author/Illustrator Teams:

Jon Scieszka and Lane Smith
Leo and Diane Dillon
Walter Dean and Christopher Myers
Andrea and Brain Pinkney
Penny Chisholm and Molly Bang
Pam Munoz Ryan and Brian Selznick
Suzanne Tripp Jurmain and Larry Day

Did you know?

Publishers usually like to have a picture book author create the text and submit it. Then an agent reads the text and matches it with an illustrator. Sometimes the author and illustrator never discuss the completed work! Sometimes there is minor conversation between the two but only through the publisher's agent. Very rarely is there collaboration.

So – that shows how very important the text of a picture book really is. With a minimal number of words, it must tell a very complete and clear story in order for the illustrator to "get it right." Picture book reviewers often talk about the symbiotic relationship between words and illustrations. One can see, perhaps, why Caldecott winners seem to be those where there is a collaboration between author and illustrator.

Picture books are for all ages and for all subjects!

This book contains reviews of 529 picture books!

Many titles are in my personal library, or I have read them at the public library or Barnes & Noble. Most all have been reviewed on Amazon.

Amazon offers the option to look inside the book and get an idea of the text and the artwork. It also provides a summary of the book as well as reviews by publishers and journals. A list of the awards each book has achieved is provided. Amazon customers who purchased the book can also leave reviews.

I have organized the titles by seven subject areas: science, math, history, language arts, the arts, character, and miscellaneous. Some categories have sub categories for further clarification.

I am particularly interested in the sophistication of many picture book titles and I have done several workshops for schools on using picture books in middle and high school. Most all of the teachers in the workshops were not aware of the complexity of the picture books available or how they can be used with older students.

Many well-known authors of books and programs regarding the teaching of reading and writing use picture books as mentor texts. It is easier to pick out examples of writers' craft in a picture book because there is much less text and there are major clues within the illustrations. This also can generate more discussions because of easier understanding. Since they are short and appealing and can be read in one sitting – they are easy to incorporate into any lesson.

Picture books are especially useful as models for writing. A wordless picture book can be used for individual students to create their own stories. The writing style used for the text can become a formula to help students develop a written story. The unusual perceptions and illustrations can spark ideas for creative writing. The illustrations are often of art gallery quality. Visual literacy - the ability to interpret, negotiate, and make meaning from information presented in the form of an image - is enhanced through the vibrant illustrations in picture books.

These particular books, including many listed here, are not suitable for the preschool - elementary school student but are more appropriate for middle and high school students. The point that is often overlooked - because it is unknown - is the sophistication, viewpoints, and perspectives of some picture books. There are those that detail the suffering of war, slavery, civil rights, immigration, poverty, homelessness, bullying, and mental illness.

Picture books can be used to:

- start a discussion about historical events
- give background information on the discovery of inventions
- give insight to famous people
- provide a better understanding of geographical locations
- develop character traits
- highlight math concepts
- embellish and enhance grammar lessons
- feature poetry styles
- bring new clarity to concerning issues
- model various types of writing
- generate ideas for creative writing
- introduce sophisticated concepts and ideas
- demonstrate succinct, rich language
- demonstrate writers craft: setting, foreshadowing, characterization, theme, plot, conflict, point of view, etc. because of brief, explicit text and supportive illustrations
- demonstrate alliteration, personification, simile, metaphor, illusion, irony, parallel structure, understatement, hyperbole, and onomatopoeia because of brief text and beautiful illustrations

Resources:

Notice & Note: Strategies for Close Reading – Beers, Kylene and Robert E. Probst. Heinemann, 2013

Routman, Regie. *Reading Essentials: The Specifics You Need to Teach Reading Well.* Heinemann, 2003.

Murphy, Patricia. *Using Picture Books to Engage Middle School Students.* Middle School Journal, March 2009 pgs 20-24.

Cochrane, Gail. *Picture Books Are Relevant for Students of ALL Ages.* Feb 5, 2018.

Ripp, Pernille. *Using Picture Books in the Middle School Classroom.* Dec 19, 2017.

Schliesman, Megan. *Never Too Old: Picture Books to Share with Older Children and Teens.* Cooperative Children's Book Center, School of Education, University of Wisconsin-Madison, 2007.

A monthly update, with many reviewed, additional titles, will be available to you if you email me at brainfitness78@gmail.com Log on to www.cognitive-fitness.com to see my other work.

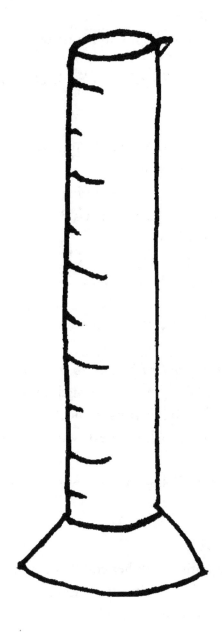

Science

SCIENCE

Rockliff, Mara. *Mesmerized: How Ben Franklin Solved a Mystery that Baffled All of France.* (2015)
- Iacopo Bruno. illustrator
- Depicts the development of the scientific method and the placebo effect
- History, critical thinking, and science
- Lush, full-color illustrations, with ribbons and curlicues

Sis, Peter. *The Tree of Life: A Book Depicting the Life of Charles Darwin: Naturalist, Geologist, & Thinker.* (2003)
- Biography of Darwin
- Explores his life, his work, and his sources of inspiration
- Illustrations of pen and ink and watercolor
- American Library Association Best Book for Young Adults
- American Library Association Notable Children's Book
- New York Times Best Illustrated Book
- New York Times Notable Children's Book
- Publishers Weekly Best Children's Book of the Year
- School Library Journal Best Book of the Year
- Bank Street - Best Children's Book of the Year

Winter, Jeanette. *The Watcher: Jane Goodall's Life with the Chimps.* (2011)
- This is the story of Jane Goodall - the observer of chimpanzees
- From her childhood in London to her years in the African forests of Gombe and Tanzania
- She was invited by brilliant scientist Louis Leakey to observe chimps
- Full-page colorful drawings
- Best Book of the Year- Boston Globe, Kirkus Reviews, Booklist, and the Bank Street College of Education

McDonnell, Patrick. *Me…Jane.* (2011)
- A story of Jane Goodall beginning with her childhood and her toy chimpanzee, Jubilee
- As a child she dreams of a life living with and helping all animals
- Pen and ink and watercolor illustrations
- 2012 Caldecott Honor Book
- Charlotte Zolotow Award Winner
- Horn Book Fanfare Book
- New York Times Best Illustrated Children's Book
- New York Times Notable Children's Book
- Booklist Editor's Choice Book
- Kirkus Reviews Best Book

SCIENCE

- Kids' Indie Next List Book
- 2011 Bank Street College Children's Book Committee Outstanding Book
- University of Wisconsin-Madison CCBC 2012 Children's Choices Book
- Parents' Choice Silver Honor Book
- National Parenting Publications Awards Gold Winner
- Booklinks Lasting Connections Book
- 2014 Illinois Monarch Children's Choice Award Winner
- 2014 Iowa Goldfinch Book Award Winner

Portis, Antoinette. *Hey, Water!* (2019)
- Everything to know about water
- Brush, sumi ink, and digital color illustrations
- Robert F. Sibert Honor Book
- American Library Association Notable Children's Book
- School Library Journal Best Book of the Year
- Bank Street Best Book of the Year
- Canadian Broadcasting Corporation Champions of Change Showcase selection

Hopkins, H. Joseph. *The Tree Lady: The True Story of How One Tree Loving Woman Changed a City.* (2013)
- Jill McElmurry, illustrator
- Katherine Olivia Sessions, first woman to graduate from the University of California, 1881
- With her science degree and her love for trees she transformed San Diego from a barren desert to a lush garden of trees
- Full-page colorful illustrations

Jenkins, Steve. *Hottest, Coldest, Highest, Deepest.* (2004)
- Some of the most amazing places on earth
- Colorful paper collages

Rosenstock, Barb. *Otis and Will Discover the Deep: The Record-Setting Dive of the Bathysphere.* (2018)
- Katherine Roy, illustrator
- June 6, 1930, engineer Otis Barton and explorer Will Beebe dove into the ocean
- They were inside a hollow metal ball of their own invention called the bathysphere
- True science adventure story
- Watercolor illustrations
- Bank Street College Best Children's Book of 2018
- American Library Association Children's Notables List 2019

- National Science Teachers Association and Children's Book Council Outstanding Science Trade Book for Students K-12
- National Science Teachers Association Best STEM Book
- Notable Social Studies Trade Books for Young People Selection 2019
- Green Earth Book Award Longlist 2019
- Cooperative Children's Book Center Choices 2019
- National Council of Teachers of English Orbis Pictus Recommended Book
- New York Public Library Best Book for Kids
- School Library Journal Best Book of 2018
- 2018 Bulletin of the Center for Children's Books - Blue Ribbon Title

Simon, Seymour. *Animals Nobody Loves.* (2002)
- 26 giant photos of nature's most gross and fierce animals

Case, Julie. *Emma and the Whale.* (2017)
- Lee White, illustrator
- A young girl helps rescue a baby whale who has washed ashore
- Watercolor and mixed media illustrations

Keating, Jess. *Pink is for Blobfish: Discovering the World's Perfectly Pink Animals.* (2016)
- Highlighting the pinkish, wildest, weirdest critters in the animal kingdom
- Cartoonish illustrations along with photos
- A New York Public Library Best Book for Kids, 2016

Roy, Katherine. *How to Be an Elephant: Growing Up in the African Wild.* (2017)
- A detailed description of the life of a baby elephant in the African wild
- Full-page watercolor illustrations
- School Library Journal Best Book of 2017
- Horn Book Fanfare Best Book of 2017
- Chicago Public Library Best Book of 2017

Garrett, Ann. *Keeper of the Swamp.* (2016)
- Karen Chandler, illustrator
- Story of protecting wildlife in the Louisiana swamps
- A boy and his ailing grandfather pole a small boat out into the Louisiana bayou where they see Boots, a female alligator the grandfather saved from poachers years ago
- The boy learns to take care of this wild creature
- Oil painting and computer imaging illustrations

SCIENCE

Demi. *Marie Curie.* (2018)
- An extraordinary scientist and winner of two Nobel Prizes
- Maria Salomea Sklodowaska was born on November 7, 1867
- She earned degrees in physics and mathematics and discovered radium and polonium
- She also coined a new word: radioactive
- Delicate, gold-accented style of artwork

Valdez, Patricia. *Joan Procter, Dragon Doctor: The Woman Who Loved Reptiles.* (2018)
- Felicita Sala, illustrator
- An internationally recognized herpetologist, she became the Curator of Reptiles at the British Natural History Museum
- Designed the Reptile House at the London Zoo and created a habitat for the Komodo Dragon
- Vibrant artwork using a variety of techniques

Keating, Jess. *Shark Lady: The True Story of How Eugenie Clark Became the Ocean's Most Fearless Scientist.* (2017)
- Marta Alvarez Miguens, illustrator
- Eugenie Clark (1922-2015) studied sharks and earned several college degrees to study them thoroughly
- She wanted people to know sharks were to be admired AND women can do anything
- Illustrations in blues and greens done in Adobe Photoshop – sharks depicted as happy, friendly creatures
- Amazon Best Book of the Month
- Best Children's Book of 2017 by *Parents* Magazine
- One of New York Times's Twelve Books for Feminist Boys and Girls

Martin, Jacqueline Briggs. *Farmer Will Allen and the Growing Table.* (2016)
- Eric-Shabazz Larkin, illustrator
- A former basketball star
- Took an abandoned lot in Milwaukee and turned it into a farm
- Named a genius problem-solver in 2008 by the MacArthur Foundation
- Used innovative urban farming methods, including aquaponics and hydroponics
- Mixed-media cityscapes
- 2014 Notable Children's Book, American Library Association
- Cooperative Children's Book Center Choices
- Best Books 2013 Nonfiction School Library Journal
- 100 Titles for Reading and Sharing 2013 New York Public Library
- Top 10 Sustainability Title 2013 Booklist
- Top 10 Crafts & Gardening Title for Youth Booklist

- 15 Books for Future Foodies Food Tank: The Food Think Tank
- Beverly Clearly Children's Choice Award 2015-2016, Oregon Association of School Libraries
- Star of The North Book Award 2015-2016, Minnesota Youth Reading Awards
- Louisiana Young Readers' Choice 2016, Louisiana Center for the Book in the State Library of Louisiana

Yaccarino, Dan. *The Fantastic Undersea Life of Jacques Cousteau*. (2012)
- A well-written and complete biography of Cousteau
- He invented so many things to make underwater exploration safer
- He also taught us about protecting the oceans
- Colorful gouache illustrations

Bathala, Dr. Neeti and Jennifer Keats Curtis. *Moonlight Crab Count*. (2017)
- Veronica V. Jones, illustrator
- Dr. Neeti Bathala is an ecologist
- Story of citizen scientists who count horseshoe crabs that visit their beach
- Contains valuable facts about these ancient animals and the effort for their conservation
- Beautiful full-page, color illustrations
- Outstanding Science Trade Book
- International Literacy Association Children's Choices Reading List

Cousteau, Philippe and Deborah Hopkinson. *Follow the Moon Home: A Tale of One Idea, Twenty Kids, and a Hundred Sea Turtles*. (2016)
- Meilo So, illustrator
- Environmental message about how kids can change the world
- Coauthor Philippe Cousteau
- Beautiful watercolor illustrations

Buzzeo, Toni. *A Passion for Elephants: The Real-Life Adventure of Field Scientist Cynthia Moss*. (2015)
- Holly Berry, illustrator
- A scientist, nature photographer, and animal-rights activist, fighting against the ivory poachers who kill elephants for their tusks
- She has spent years learning everything about these amazing creatures
- Atmospheric mixed-media illustrations, rich colors, interesting textures, patterns and vast landscapes

Kudlinski, Kathleen V. *Boy, Were We Wrong About the Weather!* (2015)
- Sebastia Serra, illustrator
- The authors share information about weather, to debunk old myths and provide the latest research
- Lively, engaging cartoon illustrations

SCIENCE

Lawlor, Laurie. *Rachel Carson and Her Book That Changed the World.* (2014)
- Laura Beingessner, illustrator
- A journalist and researcher and a major figure in the early environmental movement
- Sharing the real impact that humans have on the environment and what needs to change
- Beautiful watercolor illustrations
- National Science Teachers Association Outstanding Science Trade Book
- Bank Street Best Children's Book of the Year

Bang, Molly and Penny Chisholm. *Buried Sunlight: How Fossil Fuels Have Changed the Earth.* (2014)
- Molly Bang, illustrator
- Information about fossil fuels – she refers to coal, oil, and gas as buried sunlight
- By digging them up and burning them, we are changing the carbon balance of our air and water
- Brightly colored full-page illustrations

Bang, Molly and Penny Chisholm. *Living Sunlight: How Plants Bring the Earth to Life.* (2009)
- Molly Bang, illustrator
- About the energy we share with all living things
- Beautiful illustrations

Bang, Molly and Penny Chisholm. *Ocean Sunlight: How Tiny Plants Feed the Seas.* (2012)
- Molly Bang, illustrator
- A description of the amazing balance of life cycle and food chain within the seas
- From tiny, aquatic plants to huge whales
- Dazzling illustrations

Bang, Molly and Penny Chisholm. *Rivers of Sunlight: How the Sun Moves Water Around the Earth.* (2017)
- Molly Bang, illustrator
- The constant movement of water as it flows around the earth
- A beautifully illustrated water cycle
- Beautifully illuminated illustrations in blues, yellows, and greens

Wild, Margaret. *The Dream of the Thylacine.* (2013)
- Ron Brooks, illustrator
- Also known as the Tasmanian Tiger
- Depicts the suffering of captivity
- BBC film in 1937 – photos of the last known Thylacine in captivity presented in sepia illustrations

- Endnotes explain that the Australian animal is most likely extinct
- A heartbreaking reminder of how we treat wild animals
- Softly colorful spreads of the Thylacine free in the wild and stark sepia-toned illustrations of the animal in captivity

Aston, Dianna Hutts. *The Moon Over Star.* (2008)
- Cherise Boothe, illustrator
- Tribute to the 40th anniversary of the Apollo 11 Mission
- Also, a tribute to Mae Jemison
- Lushly illustrated

Beaty, Andrea. *Rosie Revere, Engineer.* (2013)
- David Roberts, illustrator
- Rosie wants to be an engineer
- Her Aunt Rose the riveter encourages her to keep trying and never quit
- Watercolor and ink illustrations with whimsical details
- 2013 Parents' Choice Award – GOLD
- 2014 Amelia Bloomer Project List
- ReadBoston's Best Read Aloud Book
- New York Times Bestseller
- Brown, Don. *One Giant Leap: The Story of Neil Armstrong.* (2001)
- Written on the 30th anniversary of the moon landing
- Pen and ink and watercolor illustrations

Floca, Brian. *Moonshot: The Flight of Apollo 11.* (2019)
- The story of that summer in 1968 when Apollo 11 landed on the moon
- Visually stimulating illustrations
- Robert F. Sibert Honor Book
- New York Times Best Illustrated Book

INVENTORS AND INVENTIONS

Wittenstein, Barry. *The Boo-Boos That Changed the World: A True Story About an Accidental Invention (Really!).* (2018)
- Chris Hsu, illustrator
- Story of the accidental invention of the band-aid in 1920
- Earle Dickson, a cotton buyer, worked for Johnson & Johnson
- He created bandages for his wife who was accident-prone
- Mixed media, whimsical illustrations

SCIENCE

Polivka, Jef and Rob. *A Dream of Flight: Alberto Santos-Dumont's Race Around the Eiffel Tower.* (2019)
- Rob Polivka, illustrator
- Deutsch Prize – a coveted aviation prize in Europe
- A pilot must fly a balloon from Paris's Aero Club around the Eiffel Tower and back in 30 minutes
- In 1901, Santos-Dumont was in the middle of the race when the engine on the airship he invented - died
- Pen and watercolor illustrations
- 2020 National Science Teachers Association Best STEM Book

Maurer, Tracy Nelson. *Samuel Morse, That's Who!: The Story of the Telegraph and Morse Code.* (2019)
- El Primo Ramon, illustrator
- Morse was one of the first technology pioneers
- Story tells of his inventions - the telegraph and the Morse code
- Pencil line drawings and digital color illustrations
- National Science Teachers Association Best STEM Book of the Year
- Junior Library Guild
- Bank Street College Best Book of the Year

Aronson, Sarah. *Just Like Rube Goldberg: The Incredible True Story of the Man Behind the Machines.* (2019)
- Robert Neubecker, illustrator
- A talented artist – Rube went to college to become an engineer – but did not like it
- He got a job with a newspaper and won a Pulitzer prize for his cartoons
- He became known for wild and complicated machines he created to perform simple tasks
- Colorful animated illustrations

Hood, Susan. *The Fix-It Man.* (2016)
- Arree Chung, illustrator
- Rube Goldberg inventions
- Cartoon illustrated story

Barretta, Gene. *Neo Leo: The Ageless Ideas of Leonardo da Vinci.* (2016)
- Sketches and drawings of da Vinci from over 500 years ago have been the basic ideas for many inventions
- Great information connecting da Vinci's ideas to the exact inventions
- Comical illustrations

Barretta, Gene. *Now & Ben: The Modern Inventions of Benjamin Franklin.* (2008)
- A delightful introduction to the many contributions of Ben Franklin
- Charming illustrations
- 2007 Bank Street Best Children's Book of the Year

Nettleton, Pamela Hill. *Benjamin Franklin: Writer, Inventor, Statesman.* (2003)
- Jeffrey Joseph Yesh, illustrator
- A brief biography highlighting some of the more famous events in his life
- Colorful illustrations

Barretta, Gene. *Timeless Thomas: How Thomas Edison Changed Our Lives.* (2017)
- Known as the Wizard of Menlo Park
- Despite many failures he persevered
- Besides the lightbulb he invented many other very useful things
- Watercolor illustrations

Ford, Gilbert. *The Marvelous Thing That Came from a Spring: The Accidental Invention of the Toy That Swept the Nation.* (2016)
- A spring fell from the desk of an engineer and coiled and rolled
- It became one of the most iconic toys in American history - the slinky
- Metal springs, dominoes, fuzzy pipe cleaners, and game pieces decorate the dioramic illustrations

Kelly, David A. *Miracle Mud: Lena Blackburne and the Secret Mud That Changed Baseball.* (2014)
- Oliver Dominguez, illustrator
- The story about the invention of the mud that is used to this day for softening baseballs
- Colorful, exaggerated, artful and comical paintings

Kulling, Monica. *All Aboard!: Elijah McCoy's Steam Engine.* (2013)
- Bill Slavin, illustrator
- The invention of the steam engine – by an African-American inventor
- Full page and full spread expressive watercolor illustrations

McCully, Emily Arnold. *Marvelous Mattie: How Margaret E. Knight Became an Inventor.* (2006)
- Created a guard to keep the shuttle from flying off the loom and injuring workers
- Also made the machine that makes the square bottom bags we use today
- Nicknamed the Lady Edison
- Pen and ink and watercolor illustrations
- 2007 Bank Street - Best Children's Book of the Year

SCIENCE

Reynolds, Peter and Paul. *Going Places.* (2014)
- Peter H. Reynolds, illustrator
- A celebration of creative spirit
- Instead of making a go-cart out of the kit – Maya lets her imagination soar
- Cartoon digital illustrations

Davis, Katherine Gibbs. *Mr. Ferris and His Wheel.* (2014)
- Gilbert Ford, illustrator
- Biography of engineer and inventor George Ferris
- 1893 Chicago World's Fair
- Inventor of the Ferris wheel – a mechanical marvel
- Lavish illustrations – all with a purple/wine color hue

Yolen, Jane. *My Brothers' Flying Machine: Wilbur, Orville, and Me.* (2003)
- Jim Burke, illustrator
- Celebrating the 100th anniversary of the Wright brothers' flight
- Told from the perspective of their sister, Katherine
- Beautifully composed, full-page illustrations

Coy, John. *Hoop Genius: How a Desperate Teacher and a Rowdy Gym Class Invented Basketball.* (2013)
- Joe Morse, illustrator
- True story of how Naismith, a teacher, invented basketball in 1891 at a school in Springfield, MA.
- Endnotes include the original rules of the game, for older readers
- Old-fashioned, "muscular" illustrations

McCarthy, Meghan. *Earmuffs for Everyone! How Chester Greenwood Became Known as the Inventor of Earmuffs.* (2015)
- Nonfiction – inventor of earmuffs in 1873
- Chester Greenwood & Company factory in Maine produced and shipped "Champion Ear Protectors" worldwide as recently as 1936
- Successful businessman and inventor – honored in the Smithsonian
- Acrylic, cartoon-like illustrations

Brill, Marlene Targ. *Margaret Knight: Girl Inventor.* (2014)
- Joanne Friar, illustrator
- Story of a young girl – a child laborer in a textile factory - who develops a safer loom
- Brightly colored full-page illustrations
- 2002 National Council of Social Studies/Children's Book Council Notable Trade Book

Miller, Pat. *The Hole Story of the Doughnut.* (2016)
- Vincent X. Kirsch, illustrator
- Factual story of the inventor of the doughnut
- Master mariner Hanson Crockett Gregory from Rockport, Maine in 1847 invented doughnuts to feed hungry sailors on the ship where he was a cook
- Bright, cartoon-like illustrations

Barton, Chris. *Whoosh! Lonnie Johnson's Super-Soaking Stream of Inventions.* (2016)
- Don Tate, illustrator
- Story of an African American NASA engineer who invented the super soaker
- Impressive inventor, interested in engineering at an early age
- Created homemade robots, space probes
- Colorful digital illustrations

ASTRONOMERS AND ASTRONOMY

Pettenati, Jeanne. *Galileo's Journal, 1609 to 1610.* (2006)
- Paolo Rui, illustrator
- A fictional journal with accurate biographical information from the year Galileo built his own telescope
- Lighthearted illustrations

Sis, Peter. *Starry Messenger: Galileo Galilei.* (2000)
- A genius who used his telescope to map the stars in the heavens
- This was exciting to many but to some it was frightening – many still believed that there was no universe
- Illustrations as rich and tightly woven as a tapestry
- Caldecott Honor Book

Roth Sisson, Stephanie. *Star Stuff: Carl Sagan and the Mysteries of the Cosmos.* (2014)
- He marveled at the stars as a young boy at the 1939 world's fair
- He became a well-known scientist
- Worked on the Voyager missions exploring the outermost regions of space
- Many illustrations appearing to be chalk on a dark, night sky background

Gerber, Carole. *Annie Jump Cannon, Astronomer.* (2011)
- Christina Wald, illustrator
- The biography of the woman who developed a system of classifying the stars by heat
- First woman honored at Oxford University with a doctor of science degree
- Beautiful, full-page illustrations

Hopkinson, Deborah. *Maria's Comet*. (2003)
- Deborah Lanino, illustrator
- Story inspired by Maria Mitchell – the first woman astronomer
- Illustrations - cobalt-blue nights, lit with constellations

ARCHITECTS

Harvey, Jeanne Walker. *Maya Lin: Artist-Architect of Light and Lines*. (2017)
- Tiemdow Phumiryk, illustrator
- The visionary artist-architect who designed the Vietnam Veterans Memorial Wall
- She began experimenting with light and lines early in her career
- Daughter of a poet and a clay artist
- Illustrations done with Photoshop
- An Amazon Best Book of the Year
- Chicago Public Library Best of the Best Book
- Amazon Best Book of the Month
- National Science Teachers Association Best STEM Book of the Year
- National Council for the Social Studies Notable Social Studies Trade Book for Young People
- Junior Library Guild Selection
- Washington Post Book that Can Help Build Strong Girls and Boys for Today's World
- Evanston Public Library Best Book of the Year
- Texas Topaz List Selection
- Northern California Independent Booksellers Association Book Award Nominee
- Cooperative Children's Book Center Master List Selection

Laden, Nina. *Roberto: The Insect Architect*. (2016)
- Roberto, a termite, always wanted to be an architect
- He dreams of building were not like his wood-eating family who always tore down
- He goes to a large bug city and finds like-minded bugs and builds the city of his dreams
- Collage illustrations

Winter, Jeanette. *The World Is Not a Rectangle: A Portrait of Architect Zaha Hadid*. (2017)
- Nonfiction story of the acclaimed architect's life
- As a Muslim woman, however, she faced many obstacles
- Acrylic illustrations
- A Washington Post Best Children's Book of 2017
- Parents' Choice Recommended

Going, K.I. *The Shape of the World: A Portrait of Frank Lloyd Wright.* (2017)
- Lauren Stringer, illustrator
- As a young boy he studied shapes – everywhere
- He studied architecture and became one of the most amazing architects of his time
- Acrylic, gouache, watercolor, and colored pencil illustrations

TECHNOLOGY

Robbins, Dean. *Margaret and the Moon: How Margaret Hamilton Saved the First Lunar Landing.* (2017)
- Lucy Knisley, illustrator
- Margaret was brilliant in math from an early age
- She went to MIT and then worked at NASA helping to put a man on the moon
- She handwrote code for the spacecraft's computer to solve any problems it might encounter
- Apollo 8, Apollo 9, Apollo 10, and Apollo 11 *we*re completed with the help of her code
- Colorful full-page illustrations

Robinson, Fiona. *Ada's Ideas: The Story of Ada Lovelace, the World's First Computer Programmer. (2016)*
- Biography of Ada Lovelace (1815–1852)
- Daughter of poet, Lord Byron and mathematician, Anna Isabella Milbanke
- Helped inventor Charles Babbage program his Analytical Engine – the precursor to the computer
- Intriguing stacked and photographed paper cutouts

Wallmark, Laurie. *Grace Hopper: Queen of Computer Code.* (2017)
- Katy Wu, illustrator
- A software tester, workplace jester, cherished mentor, ace inventor, avid reader, naval leader—AND rule breaker, chance taker, and troublemaker
- She coined the phrase – computer bug – it actually was a moth trapped inside a Navy computer
- Rich and colorful digital illustrations

Droyd, Ann. *If You Give a Mouse an iPhone: A Cautionary Tail.* (2014)
- A parody of *If You Give a Mouse a Cookie* imitates the look and pattern of Laura Numeroff's popular cumulative mouse tale with the substitution of an iPhone for a cookie
- Speech bubbles and full-page colorful illustrations

Diehn, Andi. *Computer Decoder: Dorothy Vaughan, Computer Scientist.* (2019)
- Katie Mazeika, illustrator
- Dorothy started out as a math teacher

- Despite being an African American woman working during the time of segregation, she rose to the level of the first black supervisor in the history of NASA
- She was an amazing computer decoder who solved problems and met challenges with determination
- Full-page color illustrations

Brown, Tami Lewis and Debbie Loren Dunn. *Instructions Not Included: How a Team of Women Coded the Future.* (2019)
- Chelsea Beck, illustrator
- Betty, Jean, and Kay used mathematics, electrical engineering, logic, and common sense to command a computer as large as a room (ENIAC) and expand and extend its capabilities
- They used outside-the-box thinking, persistence, and careful, accurate work
- Striking illustrations

Wessels, Marcie. *The Boy Who Thought Outside the Box: The Story of Video Game Inventor Ralph Baer.* (2020)
- Beatriz Castro, illustrator
- Creator of the first home video game system, Odyssey
- Family fled Nazi-Germany; Ralph used wartime technology to transform a television into a "brown box" for gaming
- He's called the "Father of Video Games"
- Colorful illustrations

Gershowitz, Jordan. *Ignore the Trolls.* (2019)
- Sandhya Prabhat, illustrator
- A fairy tale with a contemporary message about online trolls and cyber bullying
- Rich illustrations with a style from India

A monthly update, with many reviewed, additional titles, will be available to you if you email me at brainfitness78@gmail.com Log on to www.cognitive-fitness.com to see my other work.

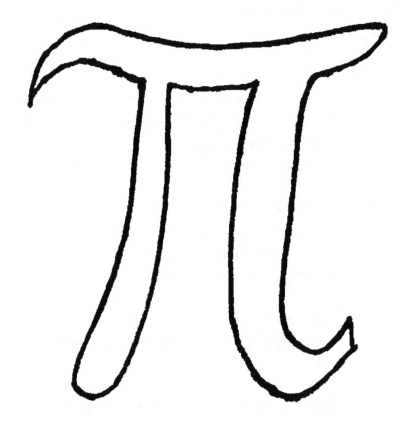

Math

MATH

Scieszka, Jon and Lane Smith. *Math Curse.* (1995)
- Whimsical story – everything becomes a math problem
- Narrator thinks she has a math curse
- Wacky collage illustrations

Adler, David A. *Millions, Billions, & Trillions: Understanding Big Numbers.* (2014)
- Edward Miller, illustrator
- Fun and creative ways to understand these numbers
- Colorful digital art illustrations

Otoshi, Kathryn. *Zero.* (2010)
- Zero sees herself as round with a hole in the center – not like the other numbers
- It is only when she learns that by joining other numbers, she becomes significant
- Great lesson about self-esteem and self-worth
- Illustrations predominantly black & white, zero is silver, other numbers are splashy colors

Shetterly, Margot Lee. *Hidden Figures: The True Story of Four Black Women and the Space Race.* (2018)
- Laura Freeman, illustrator
- The true story of Dorothy Vaughan, Mary Jackson, Katherine Johnson, and Christine Darden
- These four black women - who were excellent mathematicians – helped NASA put men in space
- Despite the odds of sexism, racism, the civil rights movement, and the space race
- Full color illustrations with diagrams, mathematical formulas, and images of outer space
- New York Times Best Seller

Slade, Suzanne. *A Computer Called Katherine: How Katherine Johnson Helped Put America on the Moon.* (2019)
- Veronica Miller Jamison, illustrator
- True story of a mathematician made famous by the film – *Hidden Figures*
- She started college at fifteen, and eventually joined NASA
- Her expertise in math helped pioneer America's first manned flight into space, its first manned orbit of Earth, and the world's first trip to the moon!
- Ink, watercolor, marker, and colored pencil illustrations

Joyce, William. *The Numberlys.* (2014)
- Christina Ellis, illustrator
- Five heroes work together to form letters from the only thing available - numbers
- Begins with black, white, gray and evolves into colors as the alphabet emerges

MATH

Helligman, Deborah. *The Boy Who Loved Math: The Improbable Life of Paul Erdos.* (2013)
- LeUyen Pham, illustrator
- At age four he had an astonishing ability in math
- He traveled around the world conversing with famous mathematicians
- Was author of many mathematical publications
- Vivid illustrations
- Kirkus Reviews Best Book of 2013
- New York Times Book Review Notable Children's Book of 2013

Bardoe, Cheryl. *Nothing Stopped Sophie: The Story of Unshakable Mathematician Sophie Germain.* (2018)
- Barbara McClintock, illustrator
- True story of Sophie Germain, a self-taught mathematician, who was the first woman to win a prize from the Paris Academy of Science
- Women were not allowed to attend university
- She secretly got class notes and submitted assignments under a male name
- She worked for six years to develop a theorem to predict patterns of vibration
- Pen and ink, watercolor, and collage illustrations
- Bank Street College Best Children's Book of 2018
- Amelia Bloomer List Selection 2019
- National Science Teachers Association and Children's Book Council Outstanding Science Trade Book for Students K-12
- National Science Teachers Association Best STEM Book
- National Council of Teachers of English Orbis Pictus Recommended Book
- Cooperative Children's Book Center Choices 2019
- Notable Social Studies Trade Books for Young People Selection 2019
- 2019 Mathical Award Winner, Grades K-2
- Booklinks Lasting Connections Pick
- Evanston Public Library Best Book for Kids

Mosca, Julia Finley. *The Girl With a Mind for Math: The Story of Raye Montague,* (2018)
- Daniel Rieley, illustrator
- True story of an African American woman who wanted to become an engineer to design ships
- It was a challenge all the way because of sexism and racial inequality
- Despite that she changed the course of ship design forever
- Digitalized illustrations
- National Science Teachers Association Outstanding Science Trade Book 2019 Selection
- National Science Teachers Association Best STEM Trade Books for Students K-12 2019
- 2019 Amelia Bloomer List Selection
- 2019 Mathical Honor Book

NEUSCHWANDER, CINDY. *SIR CUMFERENCE*

A series of picture books which are medieval stories with characters with names such as Sir Cumference, his wife Lady Di of Ameter, and their son Radius and provide a punny but practical review of math concepts for older students. Wayne Geeham, illustrator

Neuschwander, Cindy. *Sir Cumference and the First Round Table.* (1997) geometry
Neuschwander, Cindy. *Sir Cumference and the Fraction Faire.* (2017) fractions
Neuschwander, Cindy. *Sir Cumference and the Off the Charts Dessert.* (2013) charts and graphs
Neuschwander, Cindy. *Sir Cumference and the Dragon of Pi.* (1999) pi
Neuschwander, Cindy. *Sir Cumference and the Great Knight of Angleland.* (2001) angles
Neuschwander, Cindy. *Sir Cumference and the Isle of Immeter.* (2006) area and perimeter
Neuschwander, Cindy. *Sir Cumference and the Roundabout Battle.* (2015) rounding
Neuschwander, Cindy. *Sir Cumference and the Viking's Map.* (2012) coordinate geometry
Neuschwander, Cindy. *Sir Cumference and the Sword of the Cone.* (2011) geometric shapes
Neuschwander, Cindy. *Sir Cumference and All the King's Tens.* (2009) place value & counting by tens

GREG TANG

Greg Tang, a math consultant, brings colorful art, rhymes, riddles, and fun to basic math. He also provides a connection with math and science, the brain, and art masterpieces. Harry Briggs, Greg Paprocki, Heather Cahoon, Taia Morley, illustrators
www.gregtang.com.

Tang, Greg. *The Grapes of Math.* (2004)
Tang, Greg. *The Best of Times.* (2002)
Tang, Greg. *Math for All Seasons: Mind-Stretching Math Riddles.* (2005)
Tang, Greg. *Math-terpieces: The Art of Problem-Solving.* (2003)
Tang, Greg. *Math Fables: Lessons That Count.* (2004)
Tang, Greg. *Math Potatoes: Mind-stretching Brain Food.* (2005)
Tang, Greg. *Math Appeal: Mind-Stretching Math Riddles.* (2003)
Tang, Greg. *Math Fables Too: Making Science Count.* (2007)

A monthly update, with many reviewed, additional titles, will be available to you if you email me at brainfitness78@gmail.com Log on to www.cognitive-fitness.com to see my other work.

History

HISTORY

Anderson, Laurie Halse. *Thank You, Sarah: The Woman Who Saved Thanksgiving.* (2005)
- Matt Faulkner, illustrator
- Story of Sarah Josepha Hale – a lady editor who worked hard to make Thanksgiving a national holiday
- In 1863, after petitioning for 35 years – Abraham Lincoln signed the Thanksgiving Proclamation making Thanksgiving a national holiday
- Spirited and irreverent caricature illustrations

Dalgliesh, Alice. *The Thanksgiving Story.* (1985)
- Helen Sewell
- The story of passengers struggling to survive the trip on the Mayflower
- They arrive on land only to find bitter cold, no food, and much sickness
- The natives however, offer help and teach them to grow their own food
- Each year, in November, they celebrate the harvest
- Strikingly stylized, native pictures like colored etchings
- Caldecott Honor Book

Weatherford, Carol Boston. *I, Matthew Henson: Polar Explorer.* (2007)
- Eric Velasquez, illustrator
- He sailed from the port of Baltimore and survived the Arctic wilderness
- He worked with Admiral Perry for years on end
- And finally, he reached the North Pole and made history
- Including portraits and dynamic action scenes, and beautifully textured pastel illustrations

Hopkinson, Deborah. *Keep On!: The Story of Matthew Henson, Co-Discoverer of the North Pole.* (2015)
- Stephen Alcorn, illustrator
- A harrowing account of African-American explorer Matthew Henson's 1909 journey to the North Pole with Admiral Perry
- Excerpts from Henson's expedition diaries, a time line, and an epilogue place the story in its historical context
- Watercolor washes and collage-like illustrations

Weatherford, Carole Boston. *Schomburg: The Man Who Built a Library.* (2017)
- Eric Velasquez, illustrator
- Schomburg, a law clerk, of Afro-Puerto Rican descent, collected books, letters, music, and art
- These came from Africa and the African diaspora to highlight achievements of people of African descent
- Eventually, as the collection grew, he took it to the New York Public Library

- Known as Schomburg Center for Research in Black Culture - it is valued by scholars all over the world
- Oil on watercolor illustrations

Chandra, Deborah and Madeleine Comora, *George Washington's Teeth*. (2003)
- Brock Cole, illustrator
- George Washington suffered his whole life with tooth problems
- In reality – he never had wooden teeth as was often reported
- By the time he was president he only had two teeth left
- Includes a 4-page timeline of period portraits of Washington
- Humorous illustrations

Cullen, Lynn. *Dear Mr. Washington*. (2015)
- Nancy Carpenter, illustrator
- A series of letters between the daughter of the artist commissioned to paint a portrait of Washington and Washington himself
- The artists' children are rambunctious and make the sittings difficult
- They constantly remind Washington to smile
- Pen on paper, acrylic paint on canvas, and digital media illustrations

Jurmain, Suzanne Tripp. *George Did It*. (2007)
- Larry Day, illustrator
- A story based on little-known facts and told with a lot of humor
- George Washington claimed he was too nervous to be president
- His friends and supporters encouraged him and he realized that he had an important job to do and in fact – he could do it!
- Watercolor wash illustrations

Rockwell, Anne. *Big George: How a Shy Boy Became President Washington*. (2015)
- Matt Phelan, illustrator
- Great story of the whole man – George Washington – from shy boy to legendary leader
- Pencil and gouache illustrations

Eggers, Dave. *The Bridge Will Not Be Gray*. (2015)
- Nonfiction story about keeping the color of the Golden Gate Bridge - orange
- Full-page, colorful, cut-paper illustrations
- A Publishers Weekly Best Book of 2015
- A Junior Library Guild Selection
- One of Cool Mom Picks Best Children's Book of 2015

Eggers, Dave. *Her Right Foot.* (2017)
- Nonfiction story about the statue – stating that the uplifting right foot means open immigration
- Interesting I read one comment in Amazon reviews stating that this is liberal propaganda!
- Beautiful full-page colorful illustrations
- Chicago Tribune Best Children's Books of the Year
- BookPage Best Children's Books of the Year
- Mighty Girl Books of the Year
- Boston Globe Best Children's Book of the Year
- International Literacy Association Teachers Choices 2018 Reading List

Drummond, Allan. *Liberty!* (2002)
- In 1886 the statue of liberty was unveiled
- Interesting prose shared by a young boy observing the festivities
- Pen and wash illustrations

Stevenson, Harvey. *Looking at Liberty.* (2003)
- The author tells the story of the concept and the creation of the Statue of Liberty
- The statue has been an inspiration to so many
- Dramatic paintings

Yolen, Jane. *Naming Liberty.* (2008)
- Jim Burke, illustrator
- A young girl – traveling across the sea to her new homeland
- When she sees the Statue of Liberty in New York Harbor – she decides her new, American name, will be Liberty
- Luminous paintings, on burnt sienna oil-washed boards, generous use of aqua paint

Thermes, Jennifer. *Manhattan: Mapping the Story of an Island.* (2019)
- Story of 400 years of history of the island of Manhattan
- Additional information in sidebars
- Colorful illustrations including detailed maps
- Orbis Pictus Honor Book Award for Outstanding Nonfiction for Children 2020

Bunting, Eve. *Train to Somewhere.* (2000)
- Ronald Himler, illustrator
- Journey on one of the many "orphan trains" in the mid-1850s and the late 1920s
- Brought children from New York City orphanages to adoptive families in the West
- Marianne had 13 companions who were chosen for adoption at the various train stations

- Only Marianne remains and finds a new family in Somewhere, Iowa, the train's last stop
- An elderly couple, who clearly had planned on adopting a boy, take Marianne in
- Sometimes what you get turns out to be better than what you wanted in the first place
- Bordered paintings - warm colors and softly blended brush strokes

Naberhaus, Sarvinder. *Blue Sky White Stars.* (2017)
- Kadir Nelson, illustrator
- Inspiring and patriotic tribute to America – from sea to shining sea
- Amazingly beautiful full-page illustrations

Fleming, Candace. *Imogene's Last Stand.* (2014)
- Nancy Carpenter, illustrator
- Imogene loves history and takes on her hometown when the leaders decide to demolish the Historical Society in favor of a shoelace factory
- She has a very difficult time convincing the townspeople of the importance of history
- Pen and ink and digital media illustrations

Floca, Brian. *Lightship.* (2007)
- Lightships were anchored in dangerous waters where there were no lighthouses
- They provided safe passage for large ships through fog, dark night, and storms
- Last one was decommissioned in 1983
- Beautiful watercolor drawings

Floca, Brian. *Locomotive.* (2013)
- Exploration of early railroads
- Substantial introductory and ending material with details for older readers
- Bold, detailed watercolors
- Caldecott Medal Winner
- Sibert Honor Book
- New York Times Bestseller

Fulton, Kristen. *Long May She Wave: The True Story of Caroline Pickersgill and Her Star-Spangled Creation.* (2017)
- Holly Berry, illustrator
- From a family of flag makers in Baltimore
- Stitched the flag that flew over Fort McHenry
- This flag served as the inspiration for Francis Scott Key
- Blocked print art – vibrant and red, white, and blue illustrations

Garland, Michael. *Americana Adventure.* (2008)
- A new approach to the search and find game
- A treasure hunt around America – a great introduction to American history
- Combination of original artwork and photos

Garland, Michael. *The President and Mom's Apple Pie.* (2002)
- William Howard Taft makes a whistle stop to dedicate a flag in a small town
- He gets sidetracked by the delicious smells from the many cuisines available
- Humorous and campy story
- Americana style illustrations

Hopkinson, Deborah. *Abe Lincoln Crosses a Creek: A Tall, Thin Tale.* (2016)
- John Hendrix, illustrator
- Nonfiction telling a little-known story of Abe as a child
- Ink and watercolor artwork
- An American Library Association/Association for Library Service to Children Notable Children's Book
- Booklist Editors' Choice
- Bulletin Blue Ribbon Book

Jackson, Ellen. *Abe Lincoln Loved Animals.* (2008)
- Doris Ettlinger, illustrator
- A biography of Lincoln that focuses on his life-long love and compassion for animals
- Bright, cheery artwork

Kalman, Maira. *Looking at Lincoln.* (2017)
- The little girl in the story finds out many things about Abraham Lincoln
- He loved freedom, he had a dog named Fido, he loved Mozart, he kept his notes in his hat, and he loved his wife's vanilla cake
- A new and different look at an amazing man
- Bright, gouache illustrations

Rappaport, Doreen. *Abe's Honest Words: The Life of Abraham Lincoln.* (2016)
- Kadir Nelson, illustrator
- Part of the critically acclaimed Big Words series
- Lincoln was a self-educated man from the back woods
- His compassion and honesty gradually earned him the trust of many Americans
- He was president through a long and bitter civil war
- But most importantly – he wrote the Emancipation Proclamation ending slavery
- Exceptional artwork

HISTORY

Judge, Lita. *Pennies for Elephants.* (2009)
- Based on a true 1914 story of three elephants being retired from a Boston circus
- They agree to sell the elephants to the Franklin Park Zoo if the kids can raise $6000.
- And – of course – they do!
- Colorful, full-page illustrations

Jurmain, Suzanne Tripp. *Nice Work, Franklin!* (2016)
- Larry Day, illustrator
- The story of the determination of Franklin Roosevelt
- From battling polio to the Great Depression
- If you have a problem – solve it and if the solution doesn't work – try another – NEVER give up!
- Watercolor and pen and ink illustrations

Jurmain, Suzanne Tripp. *Worst of Friends: Thomas Jefferson, John Adams and the True Story of an American Feud.* (2011)
- Larry Day, illustrator
- Jefferson and Adams were good friends with widely differing political views
- They each became a leader of the opposing political party
- The story is filled with history and humor about two political rivals who put all that aside for the sake of friendship
- Watercolor and ink illustrations
- Kerley, Barbara. *Those Rebels, John & Tom.* (2012)
- Edwin Fotheringham, illustrator
- Two very different men and how they formed an alliance
- John Adams and Thomas Jefferson worked to write the Declaration of Independence with differing opinions
- Valuable lesson on working together
- Very colorful full-page illustrations
- National Council of Teachers of English Orbis Pictus Award Honor Book

Kalman, Maira. *Thomas Jefferson: Life, Liberty and the Pursuit of Everything.* (2014)
- Amazing facts about the real Thomas Jefferson
- He played violin and spoke seven languages
- He was a scientist, naturalist, botanist, mathematician, and architect
- He also started the Library of Congress
- However – although he called slavery an "abomination," he owned about 150 slaves
- Distinctive, bold-stroked gouache paintings

Turner, Ann. *When Mr. Jefferson Came to Philadelphia: What I Learned of Freedom, 1776.* (2003)
- Mark Hess, illustrator
- Told by a boy whose family owns the boarding house where Jefferson stays
- During the writing of the Declaration of Independence at the Congress in Philadelphia
- Historically accurate oil paintings

Lowell, Susan. *The Elephant Quilt: Stitch by Stitch to California!* (2008)
- Stacey Dressen-McQueen, illustrator
- Lily Rose helps her family stitch their adventures into a quilt
- They are traveling west – from Missouri to California
- Inspired by a real-life journey west in 1859
- Folk-art illustrations made to look like woodcuts

Messner, Kate. *Rolling Thunder.* (2017)
- Greg Ruth, illustrator
- Rolling Thunder Ride for Freedom – takes place every Memorial Day weekend in Washington, DC
- A boy watches his grandfather who rides his motorcycle in memory of two friends who died in Vietnam
- Realistic, colorful illustrations

Minor, Wendell. *Yankee Doodle America: The Spirit of 1776 from A to Z.* (2006)
- A journey through the America of 1776 featuring hand-painted signs
- Each sign features a person, place, or event of the time
- To follow the A to Z format the story is not chronological
- Beautiful, deep-hued oil paintings

Nelson, Kadir. *Change Has Come: An Artist Celebrates Our American Spirit.* (2009)
- A celebration of the 44th president, Barack Obama
- Illustrations in black and white

Grimes, Nikki. *Barack Obama: Son of Promise, Child of Hope.* (2008)
- Bryan Collier, illustrator
- Biography of Barack Obama
- Motivation for Americans to believe that they can change the world
- Watercolor and collage illustrations
- New York Times #1 Best Seller

Obama, Barack. *Of Thee I Sing: A Letter to My Daughters.* (2010)
- Loren Long, illustrator
- A moving tribute to 13 famous Americans whose ideals and courage shaped our country

HISTORY

- Excellent examples of valuable character traits
- Full-page, colorful illustrations

Ryan, Pam Munoz. *The Flag We Love.* (2000)
- Ralph Masiello, illustrator
- The story of the history of Old Glory
- Beautiful, vibrant illustrations

Smith, Lane. *John, Paul, George & Ben.* (2006)
- Story of the Founding Fathers as youth and their particularly childish character traits
- John Hancock, Paul Revere, George Washington, and Ben Franklin
- Wood-grain and crackle-glaze texturing, woodcut lines, and formal compositions typical of the era

Van Steenwyk, Elizabeth. *First Dog Fala.* (2008)
- Michael G. Montgomery, illustrator
- In 1940, the Scottish terrier, Fala, became the pet of President Franklin Roosevelt
- Fala traveled all over the US and the world with the president
- Portrait-like illustrations in rich colors

Van Leeuwen, Jean. *Across the Wide Dark Sea: The Mayflower Journey.* (1995)
- Thomas B. Allen, illustrator
- A young boy's personal story of the nine-week trip on the Mayflower
- Once in Plymouth Plantation, Massachusetts, they suffer through a bitter cold winter
- With the help of the natives they have a better spring and a bountiful harvest in the fall
- Soft charcoal pencil and pastels applied to textured paper

Tunnell, Michael O. *Mailing May.* (2000 – reprint edition)
- Ted Randi, illustrator
- True story set in the Idaho mountains in 1914
- No highways and a six-year-old wanting to see her grandmother 75 miles away
- Her dad has a unique solution
- Full-page color illustrations
- California Young Reader Medal Masterlist
- Colorado Children's Book Award
- 1998 American Library Association Notable Book.

Sanders, Rob. *Stonewall: A Building. An Uprising. A Revolution.* (2019)
- Jamey Christoph, illustrator
- Celebration of the 50th anniversary of the uprising at the Stonewall Inn in NYC

- First picture book to tell the true story of this incident and the gay civil rights movement
- Depicts the diverse community in the West Village
- Stirring and dynamic, full color illustrations

Robertson, David A. *When We Were Alone.* (2016)
- Julie Flett, illustrator
- A young girl learns from her grandmother about the harsh Native American boarding schools of her youth
- Warm blues and browns with splashes of red and black and white depicting the boarding school life
- 2017 Governor General's Literary Award - Young People's Literature (Illustrated Books)
- Nominated for the Toronto Dominion Canadian Children's Literature Award

Rylant, Cynthia. *Something Permanent.* (1994)
- Walter Evans, photographer
- Black and white photographs taken in the 1930's during the Great Depression
- Includes a poem about each photo

Carbone, Elisa. *Diana's White House Garden.* (2016)
- Jen Hill, illustrator
- 1943 – President Roosevelt in the White House
- Diana's dad is his chief advisor
- Diana wants to help – gets the job of starting the White House Victory Garden
- Illustration style reflects the time period - pencil, gouache, and sepia-toned backgrounds

Corey, Shana. *The Secret Subway.* (2016)
- Red Nose Studio, illustrator
- True story of New York City's first subway in 1870
- Unusual and inventive multimedia illustrations
- New York Public Library Best Book for Kids, 2016

DAVID A. ADLER – BIOGRAPHIES

A former math teacher and the author of over 260 books for kids of all ages – both fiction and nonfiction. He is best known for this biography series and the Cam Jansen series of early reader mysteries. John and Alexandra Wallner, Robert Casilla, Jeff Fisher, Dan Brown, Gershom Griffith, Collins Matt, Ronald Himler, Samuel Burd, illustrators

Adler, David A. *A Picture Book of Abraham Lincoln.* (1990)
Adler, David A. *A Picture Book of Rosa Parks.* (1993)

Adler, David A. *A Picture Book of Amelia Earhart.* 2018
Adler, David A. *A Picture Book of George Washington.* (1990)
Adler, David A. *A Picture Book of Sacagawea.* (2001)
Adler, David A. *A Picture Book of Thomas Jefferson.* (2018)
Adler, David A. *A Picture Book of Rosa Parks.* (1993)
Adler, David A. *A Picture Book of George Washington Carver.* (2000)
Adler, David A. *A Picture Book of Sojourner Truth.* (1994)
Adler, David A. *A Picture Book of Thomas Alva Edison.* (1996)
Adler, David A. *A Picture Book of Sam Houston.* (2012)
Adler, David A. *A Picture Book of John and Abigail Adams.* (2010)
Adler, David A. *A Picture Book of Lewis and Clark.* (2003)
Adler, David A. *A Picture Book of Thurgood Marshall.* (1997)
Adler, David A. *A Picture Book of John F. Kennedy.* (2018)
Adler, David A. *A Picture Book of Paul Revere.* (1997)
Adler, David A. *A Picture Book of Harriet Tubman.* (1992)
Adler, David A. *A Picture Book of Eleanor Roosevelt.* (1991)
Adler, David A. *A Picture Book of John Hancock.* (2007)
Adler, David A. *A Picture Book of Benjamin Franklin.* (2018)
Adler, David A. *A Picture Book of Samuel Adams.* (2005)
Adler, David A. *A Picture Book of Martin Luther King, Jr.* (1989

JAPANESE INTERNMENT

Bunting, Eve. *So Far from the Sea.* (2009)
- Chris K. Soentpiet, illustrator
- Laura Iwasaki and her family return to the Japanese internment camp Manzanar to pay respects to her grandfather who is buried there
- Watercolor drawings for the present and black and white drawings of the past

Uchida, Yoshiko. *The Bracelet.* (1996)
- Joanna Yardley, illustrator
- 1942 – Emi and her family are sent to an internment camp
- Emi loses the heart-shaped bracelet given to her by her best friend
- Muted, realistic paintings

Mochizuki, Ken. *Baseball Saved Us.* (1993)
- Dom Lee, illustrator
- A baseball league is formed within the confines of the internment camp
- Surrounded by barbed-wire fences and guards in towers
- Scratchboard overlays with oil illustrations

Grady, Cynthia. *Write to Me: Letters from Japanese American Children to the Librarian They Left Behind.* (2019)
- Amiko Hirao, illustrator
- Executive Order 9066 was enacted after the attack at Pearl Harbor and sent Japanese-Americans to internment camps
- Children's librarian Clara Breed's young Japanese American patrons sent to prison camp
- Librarian asks them to write to her and sent them off with books
- The Japanese American Museum has copies of some of the letters written to Ms. Breed over the three years the students were interned
- Encaustic beeswax on paper, scratching out images, and then coloring with oil paint

Yamasaki, Katie. *Fish for Jimmy: Inspired by One Family's Experience in a Japanese American Internment Camp.* (2013)
- True story of a family in a Japanese internment camp
- Younger brother Jimmy will not eat so older brother sneaks out of the camp at night to catch fresh fish for him to eat
- Exceptional, bold acrylic illustrations

Noguchi, Rick and Deneen Jenks. *Flowers from Mariko.* (2013)
- Michelle Reiko Kumata, illustrator
- After three years in a Japanese internment camp, Mariko's family is finally free to go
- They lived in a trailer park and her father's truck for his gardening business had been stolen
- Mariko plants a small garden - father finds discarded gardening tools he can repair to start again
- Characters frequently appear wooden against bleak backdrops
- Mixed media illustrations with fabrics and textures

Say, Allen. *Music for Alice.* (2004)
- Instead of going to a Japanese internment camp, Alice and her husband chose to work as farmhands
- Together, over time, they build the largest gladiola bulb farm in the country
- Sepia illustrations

Lee-Tai, Amy. *A Place Where Sunflowers Grow.* (2012)
- Felicia Hoshino, illustrator
- A story about a family in a Japanese internment camp - told in both English and Japanese
- Mari misses her home with a garden full of flowers – the camp in Topaz, Utah – a desert
- She is happy when she gets some sunflowers to grow and she attends an art class
- Earth-toned illustrations, created using watercolors, ink, tissue paper, and acrylic paint

HOLOCAUST

Elvgren, Jennifer. *The Whispering Town.* (2014)
- Fabio Santomauro, illustrator
- 1943 – a Nazi occupied small Danish fishing village is the setting
- Family shelters a Jewish family waiting for the ferry to Sweden
- Illustrations in mainly blues and grays

Deedy, Carmen Agra. *The Yellow Star: The Legend of King Christian X of Denmark.* (2020)
- Henri Sorensen, illustrator
- An unproven story of how the King of Denmark worked to keep all Danes safe from the Nazis – especially the Jews
- Full color portraits

Polacco, Patricia. *The Butterfly.* (2009)
- Set in a Nazi occupied small French village
- A girl named Sevrine is hiding from the Nazis in Monique's basement
- They become friends but the story becomes terrifying when they are discovered
- Full page illustrations

Dauvillier, Loic and Greg Salsedo. *Hidden: A Child's Story of the Holocaust.* (2010)
- Marc Lizano, illustrator
- Elsa's grandmother shares the story of her childhood in Nazi occupied Paris in 1942
- Her parents are taken away to a concentration camp - she is hidden and then adopted by neighbors
- Graphic novel
- Story is tempered by cartoon-like characters, illustrations in subdued blues and greens

Russo, Marisabina. *I Will Come Back for You: A Family in Hiding During World War II.* (2014)
- A little girl's grandmother tells the story of growing up in Rome during WW2
- Her father was taken away to a concentration camp
- She was hidden by an Italian peasant family along with her mother and siblings
- Full page color photos

Hesse, Karen. *The Cats in Krasinski Square.* (2004)
- Wendy Watson, illustrator
- A young Jewish girl and her sister fight the Nazi occupation of Warsaw
- They develop a plan to get food to those still in the Warsaw Ghetto
- Illustrations in muted tans, browns, and oranges

Polacco, Patricia. *Christmas Tapestry.* (2008)
- A roof leak damages a wall in a church and the pastor and son find a tapestry to hang on the wall and cover the damage
- A woman recognizes the tapestry and tells its story
- Then a plasterer comes to fix the wall and also recognizes the tapestry – quite an ending
- Beautiful, colorful full-page illustrations

Wild, Margaret. *Let the Celebrations Begin.* (2014)
- Julie Vivas, illustrator
- Almost overwhelming and disturbing story of women inmates at Germany's Bergen Belsen camp
- They prepare toys from scraps for a celebration when the camp is liberated
- Based on an actual account
- Haunting illustrations of concentration camp survivors

Bunting, Eve. *Terrible Things: An Allegory of the Holocaust.* (1989)
- Stephen Gammell, illustrator
- Recommended for Holocaust education
- Allegory about the events of the Holocaust using woodland animals
- Extremely moving
- All black charcoal illustrations

Johnston, Tony. *The Harmonica.* (2008)
- Ron Mazellan, illustrator
- A family is split apart when the Nazis invade Poland
- The boy plays a harmonica – a gift from his father – and is asked by a Nazi officer to play each night
- This keeps his hopes alive – an amazing story
- Dark and bleak illustrations

Gottesfeld, Jeff. *The Tree in the Courtyard: Looking Through Anne Frank's Window.* (2016)
- Peter McCarty, illustrator
- The story of Anne Frank told from the perspective of the tree in the courtyard outside the window of her secret annex
- Anne's story is told through a series of moments
- Her arrest and death are chronicled in a brief afterward
- Delicate brown illustrations
- New York Times Best Illustrated Children's Book
- New York Public Library Best Book for Kids, 2016

HISTORY

Miller, David Lee and Steven Jay Rubin. *The Cat Who Lived with Anne Frank.* (2019)
- Elizabeth Baddeley, illustrator
- Story of the time in the secret annex told by Mouschi, Peter's cat who befriends Anne
- Illustrations in ink, acrylic, pencil

Wiviott, Meg. *Benno and the Night of Broken Glass.* (2010)
- Josee Bisaillon, illustrator
- Benno, a neighborhood cat, sees the changes in German and Jewish families in Berlin
- This story takes place in the time before Kristallnacht, the Night of Broken Glass
- Great introduction to the study of the Holocaust
- Illustrations from paper, fabric, and drawings in olive, brown, and red

Tsuchiya, Yukio. *Faithful Elephants: A True Story of Animals, People, and War.* (1997)
- Ted Lewin, illustrator
- Definitely for young adults - tells the horrible consequences of war
- Japanese zoo keepers allow their three elephants to die of starvation – fearful that a bomb might set them free in the streets
- Very sad – difficult to read and even harder to forget
- Watercolor illustrations

Hoestlandt, Jo. *Star of Fear, Star of Hope.* (1996 reprint edition)
- Johanna Kang, illustrator
- Definitely for young adults
- Setting in northern France under the Nazi occupation
- In 1942, storyteller is 9 years old and finding out what is happening to her friends who wear yellow stars
- Pastel illustrations in sepia tones
- Graphics Prize at the 1994 Bologna Book Fair

Gallaz, Christophe. *Rose Blanche.* (2011)
- Roberto Innocenti, illustrator
- Good introduction to WW2 Germany from a child's view
- Somber sepia illustrations

SLAVERY

Asim, Jabari. *Fifty Cents and a Dream: Young Booker T. Washington.* (2012)
- Bryan Collier, illustrator
- Booker walked 500 miles to get to school with 50 cents in his pocket
- Watercolor collage illustrations

Turner, Ann. *My Name Is Truth: The Life of Sojourner Truth.* (2015)
- James Ransome, illustrator
- Written in the voice of Sojourner, it is a well-research biography
- She was born a slave in the late 18th century in New York
- Once free, she worked as a preacher and eventually an abolitionist
- Watercolor illustrations

Altman, Linda Jacobs. *The Legend of Freedom Hill.* (2003)
- Cornelius Van Wright and Ying-Hwa Hu, illustrators
- Story takes place in the California Gold Rush
- Rosabel, an African American, and Sophie, a Jew, search for gold
- They want to buy Rosabel's mother her freedom from a slave catcher
- Watercolor illustrations in a muted palette

Weatherford, Carole Boston. *Voice of Freedom: Fannie Lou Hamer: Spirit of the Civil Rights Movement.* (2015)
- Ekua Holmes, illustrator
- Despite being abused and very seriously beaten, Fannie was a champion for civil rights
- She was active from 1950s until her death in 1977
- During the Freedom Summer of 1964, she spoke at the Democratic National Convention
- President Johnson interfered but the speech still aired on national news on TV
- Collage illustrations
- 2016 Caldecott Honor Book
- 2016 Robert F. Sibert Honor Book
- 2016 John Steptoe New Talent Illustrator Award Winner

Turner, Glennette Tilley. *An Apple for Harriet Tubman.* (2016)
- Susan Keeter, illustrator
- As a young slave, Harriet had to work hard in her master's orchard
- She was not allowed to eat any of the apples
- When she became free – she worked very hard to help other slaves gain their freedom
- Rich, thick brushstrokes with careful use of light

Cole, Henry. *Unspoken: A Story from the Underground Railroad.* (2012) WORDLESS
- A young girl finds a runaway slave in the barn and has to decide what to do
- Somber sepia tone illustrations
- A New York Times Best Illustrated Book

Grifalconi, Ann. *Ain't Nobody a Stranger to Me.* (2007)
- Jerry Pinkney, illustrator

- Story told by a former slave to his granddaughter about his family's escape on the underground railroad
- Final notes explain the story's roots in the life of Orleans Finger, who told his story as part of the Federal Writers' Project in 1937
- Watercolor double-paged spreads contrast the sepia-toned gloomy illustrations of slavery

Meister, Carl. *Follow the Drinking Gourd: An Underground Railroad Story.* (2012)
- Robert Squier, illustrator
- An American folk song from the early 1920s
- Peg Leg Joe composed the song to guide the slaves to the underground railroad using the stars and constellations
- Eye-catching artwork

Hopkinson, Deborah. *Sweet Clara and the Freedom Quilt.* (1995)
- James Ransome, illustrator
- Story of Clara, a slave and a seamstress, on a southern plantation
- She creates a quilt out of scraps that hides a map, detailing escape information to Canada, using the underground railroad
- Full-page borderless oil illustrations

Edwards, Pamela Duncan. *Barefoot: Escape on the Underground Railroad.* (1998)
- Henry Cole, illustrator
- The adventures of a runaway slave who runs to the underground railroad to save his life
- Nocturnal illustrations

Evans, Shane. *Underground: Finding the Light to Freedom.* (2015)
- A family silently crawls through woods on a frightening journey to the underground railroad
- Dark palette until the figures reach freedom – then full color
- School Library Journal's Best Nonfiction Books of 2011

Stroud, Bettye. *The Patchwork Path: A Quilt Map to Freedom.* (2007)
- Erin Susanne Bennett, illustrator
- Hannah stitched images of signposts to guide slaves on the way to Canada using the underground railroad
- A fictionalized account of an oral history
- Oil paintings and collage illustrations
- A Gustavus Myers Center for the Study of Bigotry and Human Rights Outstanding Book, Honorable Mention
- An Oppenheim Toy Portfolio Gold Award Winner

Winter, Jeannette. *Follow the Drinking Gourd.* (2014)
- Peg Leg Joe teaches the slave children a song about the drinking gourd – the big dipper
- Slaves make the journey to freedom on the underground railroad by following the directions in the song
- Rich paintings with strong colors

Grady, Cynthia. *I Lay My Stitches Down: Poems of American Slavery.* (2012)
- Michele Wood, illustrator
- A collection of poems detailing the experiences of different slaves
- Illustrations are from quilts and various fiber art

Johnson, Angela. *All Different Now: Juneteenth, the First Day of Freedom.* (2014)
- E.B. Lewis, illustrator
- Celebration of June 19th – African American Emancipation Day
- Story includes a timeline of important events
- Rich, subdued watercolors

Levine, Ellen. *Henry's Freedom Box: A True Story from the Underground Railroad.* (2007)
- Kadir Nelson, illustrator
- Henry Brown is a young slave torn from his family and sent to work in a warehouse
- He grows up, marries, and again his family is taken from him – sold in a slave market
- In desperation, Henry mails himself to the North in a large crate and eventually finds freedom
- Powerful illustrations

Levy, Debbie. *We Shall Overcome: The Story of a Song.* (2015)
- Vanessa Brantley-Newton, illustrator
- Story of the song that has its roots in the early days of slavery
- The song continues to be the change agent in the Civil Rights Movement
- Collage illustrations

Lyons, Kelly Starling. *Hope's Gift.* (2013)
- Don Tate, illustrator
- Hope's father leaves home to join the Union army to fight for freedom
- He leaves Hope with a conch shell – the sound – he says – echoes their hope for freedom
- Upon the signing of the Emancipation Proclamation – Hope's father returns to the family
- Simple lines and soft color illustrations

Soentpiet, Chris K. *Molly Bannaky.* (2009)
- Alice McGill, illustrator
- A fictionalized story of the grandmother of Benjamin Banneker

- In the story Molly is given her freedom, acquires a cabin and turns it into a thriving 100-acre farm
- This is very unusual for a black former slave and shows her strength of character and determination
- Illustrations use space, tone, texture, and color in lighting up portions of each painting

Nelson, Vaunda Micheaux. *Almost to Freedom.* (2013)
- Colin Bootman, illustrator
- Story of slave child Lindy and her rag doll Sally and their harrowing journey to freedom
- Oil paintings in rich, dark shades

Rappaport, Doreen. *Frederick's Journey: The Life of Frederick Douglass.* (2015)
- London Ladd, illustrator
- Part of the critically acclaimed Big Words series
- Story of Fredrick Douglass from boy to man and slave to free man
- Self-educated – he wrote fervently that all people – regardless of color or gender - were entitled to equal rights
- Strong and evocative illustrations

Rappaport, Doreen. *Freedom River.* (2007)
- Bryan Collier, illustrator
- Story of John Parker – an ex-slave and successful businessman in Ohio - who repeatedly risked his life to help slaves gain freedom
- Watercolor and collage illustrations in deep blues and browns
- Coretta Scott King Illustrator Honor Book

Raven, Margot Theis. *Night Boat to Freedom.* (2008)
- E.B. Lewis, illustrator
- Granny Judith asks Christmas John to row Molly across the river
- The trip is from Kentucky to the free state of Ohio and very dangerous
- Full page illustrations in dark watercolors
- 2007 Bank Street - Best Children's Book of the Year

Smith Jr., Charles R. *Brick by Brick.* (2015)
- Floyd Cooper, illustrator
- A little-known fact – the White House was built by slaves
- Brutal work before helpful machinery was invented
- Wages were paid to their masters
- Muted but powerful illustrations

Woodson, Jacqueline. *Show Way*. (2005)
- Hudson Talbott, illustrator
- A tradition passed down through generations of slaves
- "Show ways" were quilts that hid directions and maps to help slaves find their way to freedom
- Gorgeous, multimedia art includes chalk, watercolors, and muslin
- Newbery Honor Book

Woelfle, Gretchen. *Mumbet's Declaration of Independence*. (2014)
- Alix Delinois, illustrator
- A picture book biography of Elizabeth Freeman or Mumbet, an 18th century Massachusetts's slave
- With the help of a young lawyer she challenged the Massachusetts Constitution of 1780 because it said all men are born free and equal
- Because of her hard work – in 1783 slavery was declared illegal and 5000 slaves were set free
- Vividly colored illustrations

Hamilton, Virginia. *The People Could Fly: American Black Folktales*. (1993)
- Leo and Diane Dillon, illustrators
- Fantasy tale of slaves with magical powers of the imagination as they endured the life of slavery
- Powerful illustrations
- Coretta Scott King Award
- Booklist Children's Editors' Choice
- School Library Journal Best Books of the Year
- Horn Book Fanfare
- American Library Association Notable Book
- National Council of Teachers of English Teachers' Choice
- New York Times Best Illustrated Children's Books of the Year

Ransome, James. *The Bell Rang*. (2019)
- A slave family awakens each day when the bell rings
- Mom cooks, Dad gathers wood, while Ben and his sister go out to work
- The heat is unbearable and the work is backbreaking
- One morning when the bell rings – they find that Ben is gone and they hope he will find freedom
- Full-page, brilliantly colored illustrations
- Bright, colorful illustrations
- Coretta Scott King Illustrator Honor Award
- A Kirkus Reviews Best Picture Book of 2019

Lasky, Kathryn. *A Voice of Her Own: The Story of Phillis Wheatley, Slave Poet.* (2012)
- Paul Lee, illustrator
- In 1761, a slave girl arrived from Africa to be sold to the Wheatley family in Boston
- She left her family, her name, and her language but she had a great desire to learn
- She wrote poetry, had a book of poems published, and became the first African-American woman poet
- Carefully researched paintings/illustrations

Williams, Sherley Anne. *Working Cotton.* (1997)
- Carole Byard, illustrator
- The life of a cotton picker told through the eyes of a child
- Impressionistic paintings
- Caldecott Honor Book

CIVIL RIGHTS

Levinson, Cynthia. *The Youngest Marcher: The Story of Audrey Faye Hendricks, a Young Civil Rights Activist.* (2017)
- Vanessa Brantley-Newton, illustrator
- The youngest known child to be arrested for a civil rights protest in Birmingham, Alabama, 1963
- Her preacher called for marchers and for people to picket the white stores
- She was nine years old and proved you are never too young to fight for what you believe
- Bright, digitally assembled collages

Woodson, Jacqueline. *This Is the Rope: A Story from the Great Migration.* (2017)
- James Ransome, illustrator
- The story of one family's journey north during the Great Migration – a journey made by more than six million African Americans
- The rope follows several generations – where it is used as a jump rope, a clothesline, and to tie luggage to the top of a car
- Oil illustrations

Lawrence, Jacob. *The Great Migration: An American Story.* (1993)
- After WWI large numbers of African-Americans left the southern states in the hopes of finding jobs and better living in the industrial cities of the northern states
- The people find overcrowded living conditions, poor working conditions, prejudice, and racism
- Featuring a famous sixty-panel painting of the migration
- American Library Association Notable Book

- American Library Association Booklist Editors' Choice
- International Reading Association/Children's Book Council Teachers' Choice
- Notable Children's Trade Book in the Field of Social Studies (National Council for the Social Studies/Children's Book Council)
- Carter G. Woodson Outstanding Merit Book

Woodson, Jacqueline. *The Other Side.* (2001)
- E.B. Lewis, illustrator
- Two young girls, one black and one white, are separated by a fence
- They are told - because of segregation rules – not to cross to the other side
- They develop their friendship sitting on the fence together
- Watercolor illustrations

Wittenstein, Barry. *A Place to Land: Martin Luther King Jr. and the Speech That Inspired a Nation.* (2019)
- Jerry Pinkney, illustrator
- Description of the events leading up to and the development of the famous speech
- Collage, pencil, and watercolors
- Orbis Pictus Award for Outstanding Nonfiction for Children 2020
- Selected for the Texas Bluebonnet Master List
- An American Library Association Notable Children's Book
- A Capitol Choices Noteworthy Title
- Nominated for a National Association for the Advancement of Colored People Image Award
- A Bank Street Best Book of the Year
- A Notable Social Studies Trade Book for Young People
- A Booklist Editors' Choice
- Named a Best Book of the Year by Publishers Weekly, Kirkus Reviews, and School Library Journal
- Selected for the Canadian Broadcasting Corporation Champions of Change Showcase

Asim, Jabari. *Preaching to the Chickens: The Story of Young John Lewis.* (2016)
- E.B. Lewis, illustrator
- On the family farm young John is put in charge of the flock of chickens
- He wants to be a preacher so he practices on his flock of chickens
- Full-page watercolor illustrations
- New York Times Best Illustrated Book

Bildner, Phil. *The Soccer Fence: A Story of Friendship, Hope, and Apartheid in South Africa.* (2014)
- Jesse Joshua Watson, illustrator
- Hector dreams of playing soccer on a real pitch

- In his Johannesburg township – apartheid makes that impossible
- When Mandela is released from prison apartheid begins to crumble
- When the Bufana Bufana soccer team wins the African Cup of Nations – Hector knows his dream will come true
- Acrylic and pencil illustrations

Johnson, Angela. *A Sweet Smell of Roses.* (2007)
- Eric Velasquez, illustrator
- The smell of roses is a metaphor for freedom
- Story about segregation and large groups walking for freedom
- Brown, gray, and black illustrations

Ramsey, Calvin Alexander and Bettye Stroud. *Belle: The Last Mule at Gee's Bend: A Civil Rights Story.* (2017)
- John Holyfield, illustrator
- In Gee's Bend, Alabama – the authorities set up long detours to keep African Americans from voting
- Belle was one of the mules that helped citizens get through the long journey to vote
- Beautiful, full-page, brightly colored illustrations

Bandy, Michael S. and Eric Stein. *White Water.* (2015)
- Shadra Strickland, illustrator
- A young black boy in 1962 goes to a coloreds drinking fountain on a hot day and the water is gritty and bad tasting
- He can only imagine how much better the water in the drinking fountain for whites must taste
- A good introduction to segregation in the south and the beginnings of the civil rights movement
- Mixed media illustrations

Wittenstein, Barry. *Waiting for Pumpsie.* (2017)
- London Ladd, illustrator
- Story of Pumpsie Green - the first black player on the Boston Red Sox team in 1959
- Fictionalized story about a real ball player – focusing on the family longing for an end to segregation
- Vibrant illustrations in acrylic paint

Pinkney, Andrea Davis. *Sit-In: How Four Friends Stood Up by Sitting Down.* (2010)
- Brian Pinkney, illustrator
- Celebration of the 50th anniversary of the Woolworth (Greensboro, NC) lunch counter sit-in by four black college students
- Includes a civil rights timeline

- Double-page spreads in watercolor and thick ink lines
- Jane Addams Honor Book

Shange, Ntozake. *We Troubled the Waters.* (2009)
- Rod Brown, illustrator
- Struggles of the Civil Rights movement
- Heavy issues: voting rights, Jim Crow, lynching, KKK, etc.
- Famous people: Rosa Parks, Booker T. Washington, Malcolm X, Martin Luther King
- Stunning art work – powerful and emotional

Bass, Hester. *Seeds of Freedom: The Peaceful Integration of Huntsville, Alabama.* (2018)
- E.B. Lewis, illustrator
- Little-known story about black and white citizens in a small Alabama town working together to end segregation
- Watercolor illustrations

Newton, Vanessa. *Let Freedom Sing.* (2009)
- There is an introduction by Ruby Bridges
- Story is told to the tune of "This Little Light of Mine"
- Mixed-media, electric-hued digital illustrations

Coles, Robert. *The Story of Ruby Bridges.* (2010)
- George Ford, illustrator
- First African American child to integrate a New Orleans school in 1960
- Federal marshals escorted 6-year old Ruby into the school while angry mobs of white parents protested
- Those parents kept their kids home - Ruby learned to read in an empty classroom in an empty school
- By the time Ruby was in second grade – things were back to normal
- Watercolors mixed with acrylic ink

Nelson, Vaunda Micheaux. *The Book Itch: Freedom, Truth and Harlem's Greatest Bookstore.* (2015)
- R. Gregory Christie, illustrator
- 1930s opening of the National Memorial African Bookstore – the first of its kind
- Specializing in African American history
- Place to come and read and exchange ideas – visited by many famous people
- Bold, colorful illustrations

HISTORY

Tonatiuth, Duncan. *Separate Is Never Equal: Sylvia Mendez and Her Family's Fight for Desegregation.* (2014)
- 1947 California ruling against public-school segregation
- Sylvia Mendez's family began to fight for integrated schools
- It was a hard-won victory against discrimination
- Multimedia illustrations
- Jane Addams Award Book

Ramsey, Calvin Alexander and Gwen Strauss. *Ruth and the Green Book.* (2010)
- Floyd Cooper, illustrator
- *The Green Book* (historical fact) helped a generation of African American travelers
- Listed all the places that would welcome black travelers

Barton, Chris. *The Amazing Age of John Roy Lynch.* (2015)
- Don Tate, illustrator
- In-depth look at the Reconstruction period after the Emancipation Proclamation
- Biography of the first African-American congressman
- For older readers – informative timeline and endnotes
- Cartoon-style illustrations

Sanders, Nancy I. *D Is for Drinking Gourd: An African American Alphabet.* (2007)
- E.B. Lewis, illustrator
- Each letter of the alphabet celebrating African American achievements throughout American history
- Beautiful watercolor paintings

Clinton, Catherine. *When Harriet Met Sojourner.* (2007)
- Shane W. Evans, illustrator
- Two women – both slaves
- Both fought for African American rights
- In 1864 they came together to work together
- Full-page colorful illustrations mostly browns, oranges, and yellows

Evans, Shane W. *We March.* (2016)
- August 28, 1963 – 250,000 people gathered to march on Washington for jobs and freedom
- From the Washington Monument to a rally at the Lincoln Memorial, where Martin Luther King Jr. delivered his historic "I Have a Dream" speech
- Full-page, substantial illustrations
- Kirkus Reviews' Best Children's Books of 2012

Farris, Christine King. *My Brother Martin: A Sister Remembers Growing Up with the Rev. Dr. Martin Luther King Jr.* (2006)
- Chris Soentpiet, illustrator
- Written by the older sister of Dr. King
- Describes how he grew up wanting to change the way blacks were treated
- Realistic, light-filled watercolor illustrations

Watkins, Angela Farris. *My Uncle Martin's Big Heart.* (2012)
- Eric Velasquez, illustrator
- A personal story of Martin Luther King Jr. told by his niece
- A rare glimpse of his life at home with family members
- Realistic and warm illustrations

Dray, Philip. *Yours for Justice, Ida B. Wells: The Daring Life of a Crusading Journalist.* (2008)
- Stephen Alcorn, illustrator
- Ida uses her position as a journalist to fight for civil rights
- Her greatest challenge comes when one of her friends is lynched
- Ink and watercolor illustrations

Haskins, Jim. *Delivering Justice: W.W. Law and the Fight for Civil Rights.* (2008)
- Benny Andrews, illustrator
- Story of a mail carrier who organized the Savannah Boycott
- As a result – Savannah became the first city in the south to ban racial discrimination
- Dramatic realism and folk-art combination illustrations

Hopkinson, Deborah. *Steamboat School.* (2016)
- Ron Husband, illustrator
- The story of a determined Mississippi school teacher who refused to let an unfair law keep him from teaching his students
- He started a school on a steamboat – on the Mississippi River out of the jurisdiction of the law
- There he taught his African-American students
- Pen and ink illustrations in browns and blacks

Kittinger, Jo S. *Rosa's Bus: The Ride to Civil Rights.* (2017)
- Stephen Walker, illustrator
- The story of Rosa Parks from the viewpoint of the bus
- After the incident – the bus was sold at auction
- It is now on display at the Henry Ford Museum
- Double-page, large-scale oil paintings

Reynolds, Aaron. *Back of the Bus*. (2013)
- Floyd Cooper, illustrator
- When Rosa Parks refused to give up her seat
- Perspective from a little boy seated at the back of the bus
- Beautifully illustrated

Meyer, Susan Lynn. *New Shoes*. (2016)
- Eric Velasquez, illustrator
- Ella Mae needs new shoes but has to wait until there are no white customers in the store
- Her mother traces her feet on paper and the clerk brings shoes he thinks will fit
- She cannot try them on
- Ella Mae and her friend set out to make changes in shoe shopping so there will be no more humiliation
- Realistic oil paintings

Shelton, Paula Young. *Child of the Civil Rights Movement*. (2013)
- Raul Colon, illustrator
- Written by the daughter of civil rights activist Andrew Young
- Paula joined in the historic march from Selma to Montgomery
- Colorful illustrations
- Bank Street College of Education Best Children's Book of the Year

Smith Jr., Charles R. *28 Days: Moments in Black History that Changed the World*. (2015)
- Shane W. Evans, illustrator
- Each of the 28 days features a famous black person in history
- Beginning with Crispus Attucks and ending with United States President Barack Obama
- Vibrantly colorful full-page illustrations

IMMIGRANTS, REFUGEES, MIGRANT WORKERS

Buitrago, Jairo. *Two White Rabbits*. (2015)
- Rafael Yocktang, illustrator
- A young girl tells of her travels with her father as they escape Mexico or Central America
- They ride on the top of a train, walk, hitch rides – trying to get to the border and a better life
- Digitally created illustrations full of expression
- Kirkus Reviews Best Picture Book of the Year
- School Library Journal Best Picture Book of the Year
- National Council of Teachers of English Charlotte Huck Award for Outstanding Fiction for Children Recommended Book
- United States Board on Books for Young People Outstanding International Book

- Bank Street College of Education Best Children's Book of the Year
- Notable Books for a Global Society

Del Rizzo, Suzanne. *My Beautiful Birds.* (2017)
- A story about a young boy who must leave his home during the Syrian civil war
- He leaves everything behind including his pet pigeons
- He settles into a refugee camp but is devastated by the loss of his pigeons
- Polymer clay, plasticine, and acrylic paint illustrations
- 2017 New York Times Notable Children's Books
- 2017 Malka Penn Award for Human Rights in Children's Literature Winner
- 2018 Society of Children's Book Writers and Illustrators Crystal Kite Award for Canada
- 2017 One Book for Kids, One San Diego
- 2018 Marilyn Baillie Picture Book Award finalist
- 2018 Ruth and Sylvia Schwartz Children's Book Award shortlist
- 2018 Ezra Jack Keats Book Award nominee
- 2017 Middle East Book Award: Picture Books Honor Book
- 2017 Foreword INDIES (Independent Booksellers): Picture Books finalist
- 2017 Cybils Award: Fiction Picture Book nominee
- 2017 New York Public Library's Best Books for Kids & Teens
- 2017 Stacked Books Monthly Giving: International Refugee Assistance Project
- 2018 Notable Books for a Global Society
- 2018 Canadian School Libraries Journal: Resource Links Highlights: Refugees and Immigrants
- 2018 School Library Journal blog The Classroom Bookshelf: Global Literature to Teacher Global Understanding
- 2018 Canadian Children's Book Centre Best Books for Kids & Teens Starred Selection
- 2017 New England Children's Booksellers Advisory Council Windows & Mirrors Fall
- 2017 UNICEF USA Voice The Perfect Gift for the Holidays: Books That Inspire
- 2017 School Library Journal blogger Betsy Bird's The Refugee Children's Books of 2017 and an Ode to The Arrival
- 2017 Quill & Quire Books of the Year
- 2017 Junior Library Guild selection

Roberts, Ceri. *Refugees and Migrants.* (2016)
- Hanane Kai, illustrator
- Part of a series on difficult issues children face
- Author is a journalist and free-lance writer
- Sensitive and striking illustrations

Phi, Bao. *A Different Pond.* (2017)
- Thi Bui, illustrator
- Bittersweet story about refugees from Vietnam
- Illustrator writes graphic novels, author is a poet
- Striking, evocative art
- 2018 Caldecott Honor Book

Faruqi, Reem. *Lailah's Lunch Box: A Ramadan Story.* (2015)
- Lea Lyon, illustrator
- Lailah is a student in a new country and is finally old enough to participate in Ramadan fasting
- Her teacher and the librarian help her to explain her culture to her classmates
- Full-page watercolor illustrations include some decorative arabesque borders
- 2019 Daybreak Children's Picture Book Award -- Recognizing Muslim Women's Contributions to Literature
- Notable Social Studies Trade Book for Young People 2016, a cooperative Project of the National Council for the Social Studies (NCSS) and the Children's Book Council
- Featured Book of the Month, Anti-Defamation League
- American Library Association Notable Book for Children 2016
- Skipping Stones Honor 2016
- International Literacy Association Choices Reading List

Mobin-Uddin, Asma. *My Name Is Bilal.* (2005)
- Barbara Kiwak, illustrator
- A young Muslim boy and his sister are new to the country and new to school
- Bilal sees his sister being bullied and decides thinks he should tell his classmates that his name is Bill
- One of his teachers is Muslim and gives him a book about a famous Muslim whose name was Bilal
- Watercolor illustrations

Lofthouse, Liz. *Ziba Came on a Boat.* (2007)
- Robert Ingpen, illustrator
- A mother and daughter leave their homeland and all their possessions and travel to a new, unknown land on a rickety old boat
- A story of fear and hope
- Watercolor illustrations

Bunting, Eve. *One Green Apple.* (2006)
- Ted Lewin, illustrator
- A Muslim girl in a new school in a new country has difficulty connecting with her classmates
- Things change for the better on a field trip to an apple orchard where the class makes cider
- Watercolor illustrations

Sanna, Francesca. *Me and My Fear.* (2008)
- Young adult audience
- Girl is frightened when moving to a new country
- Story provides a way to overcome the fear
- Collage illustrations

Sanna, Francesca. *The Journey.* (2016)
- Story of a family's dangerous journey from a war zone to a new country
- Effective use of oranges, pinks, and black in the illustrations
- 2017 Ezra Jack Keats New Author Honor and New Illustrator Honor Awards
- Association for Library Service to Children Notable Children's Book of 2017
- 2017 United States Board on Books for Young People Outstanding International Books
- Cooperative Children's Book Center Choices 2017
- New York Times' Notable Children's Book of 2016
- Wall Street Journal's Best Children's Books of 2016
- Publisher's Weekly's Best Books of 2016
- Kirkus Reviews' Best Picture Books of 2016
- School Library Journal's Best Picture Books of 2016
- Guardian's Best Children's Books of 2016
- New York Public Library's Best Books for Kids 2016
- All the Wonders' Best Picture Books of 2016
- Let's Talk Picture Books' Best Picture Books of 2016
- Chickadee Lit's Picture Books to Celebrate Kindness

Landowne, Youme. *Mali Under the Night Sky: A Lao Story of Home.* (2010)
- True story of Laotian American artist Malichansouk Kouanchao
- Her family was forced by civil war to flee Laos and in the new country they are jailed
- This is a story about the difficulties faced by refugees during wartime
- Watercolor wash illustrations and intricate borders
- 2011 Skipping Stones Honor Book

Shea, Peggy Dietz. *The Whispering Cloth: A Refugee's Story.* (1996)
- Anita Riggio, illustrator
- This story is set in Ban Vinai, a refugee camp in Thailand – Mai is there with her grandmother

- The widows all stitch brightly colored story cloths - Mai wants to make one - but has no story
- Close-up photos of story cloth needlework

Avi. *Silent Movie.* (2003)
- C,B, Mordan, illustrator
- In 1909 Papa sails from Sweden to New York to start a new life for his family
- Six months later, he sends for wife and son, Gustave to join him- but they get lost
- Mama finds a sweatshop job and Gustave gets a part in a silent movie and eventually Papa finds them
- The whole story is done in black and white horizontal frames like a silent movie

Barroux. *Welcome.* (2016)
- Inspired by the Syrian refugee crisis to encourage inclusiveness
- Three polar bears floating on an ice floe are looking for a new home
- No one allows them to stay – they finally find an empty island
- Then three homeless monkeys arrive and they let them stay
- Full-page color illustrations of mostly shades of blue

Bunting, Eve. *A Picnic in October.* (2004)
- Nancy Carpenter, illustrator
- An Italian-American family living in New York make a trip to the Statue of Liberty each year on October 28th to celebrate Lady Liberty's birthday
- Tony thinks it is silly – too long, too cold, and just embarrassing to have a picnic with a birthday cake on Liberty Island
- Then he meets a new family who has recently arrived in the US and learns how important the Statue of Liberty is to his immigrant grandparents
- Full-page colorful illustrations

Cutler, Jane. *Guttersnipe.* (2009)
- Emily Arnold McCully, illustrator
- Set in Canada in the early 20th century, a Jewish immigrant family is struggling, so the son gets a job making deliveries on a bike
- He has an accident and instead of being disheartened – he finds a new job
- Detailed ink and watercolor illustrations

Kobald, Irena. *My Two Blankets.* (2015)
- Freya Blackwood, illustrator
- A multicultural story about moving to a new country where everything is strange
- A story of change, sadness, and then friendship
- Combination of watercolor and oil illustrations

Polacco, Patricia. *The Blessing Cup.* (2013)
- An autobiographical story of a teacup from the hands of her great-great grandmother in Russia
- To the hands of her own children today
- Highlights the importance of family during the plight of Jewish people in the early 1900s
- Illustrations all in charcoal with the exception of color for the cup and grandma's babushka
- New York Times Best Seller

Polacco, Patricia. *Fiona's Lace.* (2014)
- An autobiographical story of Irish Fiona Hughes who makes lace
- A story of a family immigrating from Ireland to Chicago and the importance of Fiona's lace
- Pencil and acetone marker illustrations

Polacco, Patricia. *The Keeping Quilt.* (2001)
- The story of a quilt created from scraps of clothes from family members back in the Russian homeland
- The quilt has existed for four generations and is a remembrance of the family
- It is used as a Sabbath table cloth, a wedding canopy, and a blanket for newborns
- Charcoal drawings with only the quilt in splashes of color

Ringgold, Faith. *We Came to America.* (2016)
- The story reminds us that immigration has brought us many people from many countries
- These people bring languages, art, talents, history, and determination - we are better for their contributions
- Vibrant paint on canvas
- 2017 Notable Social Studies Trade Book for Young People

Yaccarino, Dan. *All the Way to America: The Story of a Big Italian Family and a Little Shovel.* (2014)
- The author's great-grandfather arrived in New York Harbor with a small shovel with this advice: work hard, enjoy life, but never forget your family
- The shovel was handed down over four generations of this Italian-American family
- Full page brightly colored illustrations

Tan, Shaun. *The Arrival.* (2007) WORDLESS
- All of the frightening possibilities faced by immigrants in a new country
- Journey of one man, threatened by dark shapes that cast shadows on his family's life, to a new country
- For middle and high school readers
- Beautiful sepia pictures, soft brushstrokes and grand Art Deco style architecture
- New York Times Best Illustrated Book
- Book Sense Book of the Year -- Honor Book
- World Fantasy Award -- Best Artist

HISTORY

- American Library Association Top Ten Great Graphic Novel for Teens
- Horn Book Fanfare Best Book
- Publishers Weekly Best Book
- New York Magazine's Top Comic Book
- School Library Journal Best Book

McCarney, Rosemary. *Where Will I Live?* (2017)
- A photo essay of thousands of young children who have been forced to flee their homeland
- The message is that children are resilient and can face the future with optimism
- Photo essay

Wild, Margaret. *The Treasure Box.* (2017)
- Frey Blackwood, illustrator
- When the library is bombed and burned and the family must flee – the treasure box that they bring contains remembrances of the family history
- Pencil, watercolor, and collage illustrations, with three-dimensional quality

Williams, Karen Lynn and Khadra Mohammed. *Four Feet, Two Sandals.* (2007)
- Doug Chayka, illustrator
- Relief workers bring boxes of clothes and two girls each find a sandal that together make a pair
- They decide it is better to share and be friends while they wait to go to America
- Warm color illustrations with sensitive brush strokes

Bunting, Eve. *How Many Days to America: A Thanksgiving Story.* (1990)
- Beth Peck, illustrator
- A family flees their native country (a small Caribbean island) in a small fishing boat and lands in the United States on Thanksgiving Day
- Full-page illustrations in dark browns and blues

Woodruff, Elvira. *Small Beauties: The Journey of Darcy Heart O'Hara.* (2006)
- Adam Rex, illustrator
- A heartwarming story of an Irish family's emigration to America during the potato famine
- Warm, colorful oil paintings

Surat, Michele Maria. *Angel Child, Dragon Child.* (1989)
- Dinh Mai Vo, illustrator
- Ut, a young Vietnamese refugee, comes to the US without her family
- She is bullied at her school and is very unhappy
- In the end the bully is the one who helps her
- Muted watercolor illustrations

Tran, Truong. *Going Home, Coming Home.* (2012)
- Ann Phong, illustrator
- Ami Chi goes to Vietnam to visit her grandmother with her parents who have not been back to Vietnam since the war
- Ami Chi likes her grandmother's house and village and even finds a friend
- Richly colored double page acrylic illustrations

Wong, Janet S. *Apple Pie Fourth of July.* (2006)
- Margaret Chodos-Irvine, illustrator
- Story of how difficult it is for children to connect two cultures
- For 4th of July a neighbor bakes apple pie but her family still prepares Chinese food which just doesn't seem appropriate for the holiday
- Brightly colored full-page illustrations

Say, Allen. *The Favorite Daughter.* (2013)
- Story of a Japanese American child - embarrassed by her name and teased by her classmates
- Her dad reminds her of her culture and heritage and encourages her to be proud of it
- Reminiscent of author Allen Say and his daughter
- Watercolor, ink, and pencil illustrations

Morales, Yuyi. *Dreamers.* (2018)
- In 1994, the author left her home in Mexico and came to the US with her infant son
- It was not easy - Yuyi spoke no English
- They found an unexpected, unbelievable place: the public library
- Mixed-media illustrations created through painting, drawing, photography, and embroidery
- Pura Belpré Illustrator Award
- New York Times / New York Public Library Best Illustrated Book of 2018
- Flora Stieglitz Strauss Award
- 2019 Boston Globe - Horn Book Honor Recipient
- Anna Dewdney Read Together Honor Book
- Best Book of 2018 by Kirkus Reviews, Publishers Weekly, School Library Journal, Shelf Awareness, National Public Radio, the Boston Globe, the Chicago Tribune, Salon.com, and many more!
- Junior Library Guild selection
- Eureka! Nonfiction Honoree
- Bulletin of the Center for Children's Books Blue Ribbon Title
- Bank Street Best Children's Book of the Year
- Children's Literature Assembly Notable Children's Book in Language Arts
- Selected for the Canadian Broadcasting Corporation Champions of Change Showcase

HISTORY

Adler, David A. and Michael S. Adler. *A Picture Book of Cesar Chavez.* (2010)
- Marie Olofsdotter, illustrator
- A biography of a Mexican-American labor leader and civil rights activist
- During the Great Depression, he worked as a produce-picker with his family in California
- He dedicated the rest of his life to helping farm laborers get better pay and working conditions
- Lively, earth-toned illustrations with folk-art backgrounds

Perez, L. King. *First Day in Grapes.* (2014)
- Robert Casilla, illustrator
- Migrant farmworker family moves to California to harvest grapes
- Chico starts third grade and finds self-confidence and good math skills help him settle in
- Brightly colored illustrations
- Pura Belpre Honor Book

Warren, Sarah E. *Dolores Huerta: A Hero to Migrant Workers.* (2012)
- Robert Casilla, illustrator
- A teacher, a mother, and a friend to migrant farmworkers
- She fights for the families to have better wages and safer working conditions
- Vibrant watercolor and pastel illustrations
- Jane Addam's Children's Honor Book for Younger Children

WOMEN IN HISTORY

Markel, Michelle. *Brave Girl: Clara and the Shirtwaist Makers' Strike of 1909.* (2013)
- Melissa Sweet, illustrator
- True story of Ukrainian immigrant Clara Lemlich
- She led the largest strike of women workers in U.S. history
- She began by going to night school, studying English, and working in a shirtwaist factory
- Describes the plight of immigrants in the early 1900s
- Collage of watercolor, gouache, blank dress-pattern paper, bookkeeping pages, stitches, and fabric pieces
- Bank Street Flora Stieglitz Straus Award
- Jane Addams Children's Book Award for Younger Children
- NCTE Orbis Pictus Honor Book

Annino, J. J. *She Sang Promise: The Story of Betty Mae Jumper, Seminole Tribal Leader.* (2010)
- Lisa Desimini and Moses Jumper, illustrators
- First female leader of the Seminole Tribe
- Born in 1923, the child of a mixed marriage so she was treated as an outsider
- She left to go to school and returned as a qualified nurse

- She was a storyteller, and activist for her people, and a journalist
- Colorful illustrations

Rockliff, Mara. *Around America to Win the Vote: Two Suffragists, a Kitten, and 10,000 Miles.* (2016)
- Hadley Hooper, illustrator
- April 1916, Nell Richardson and Alice Burke set out from New York City
- Quest: voting rights for women
- Pencil and printmaking technique illustrations

Stone, Tanya Lee. *Who Says Women Can't Be Doctors?: The Story of Elizabeth Blackwell.* (2018)
- Marjorie Priceman, illustrator
- In the 1830s women had very few career choices: wives, mothers, teachers, seamstresses – that's it
- Blackwell faced much opposition but, in the end, graduated from medical school and had a brilliant career as a doctor
- Full-page illustrations
- National Public Radio Best Book of 2013

Ryan, Pam Munoz. *Amelia and Eleanor Go for a Ride.* (1999)
- Brian Selznick, illustrator
- Story based on excerpts from diaries, book transcripts and newspaper accounts
- Two friends leave a formal dinner at the White House in 1933 to take a plane from DC to Baltimore
- Graphite and colored pencil illustrations

Wallner, Alexandra. *Betsy Ross.* (1994)
- Story of Betsy who ran an upholstery business and reportedly designed the first American flag
- Folk-style illustrations

Wallner, Alexandra. *Susan B Anthony.* (2012)
- During this time women could not vote or own property
- Her work for change was not popular
- She was one of the first on the path to the 19th amendment
- Beautiful paintings

Weatherford, Carole Boston. *Voice of Freedom: Fannie Lou Hamer, Spirit of the Civil Rights Movement.* (2015)
- Janina Edwards, illustrator
- A champion of equal voting rights
- Collage illustrations
- 2016 Caldecott Honor Book

- 2016 Robert F. Sibert Informational Book Honor Book
- 2016 John Steptoe New Talent Illustrator Award Winner

Hannigan, Kate. *A Lady Has the Floor: Belva Lockwood Speaks Out for Women's Rights.* (2018)
- Alison Jay, illustrator
- Biography of Belva Lockwood, a lawyer, activist, and presidential candidate
- Spent her life demanding equality for women
- Oil illustrations with a crackle varnish, with a look reminiscent of 19th-century folk art

Barton, Chris. *What Do You Do with a Voice Like That? The Story of Extraordinary Congresswoman Barbara Jordan.* (2018)
- Ekua Holmes, illustrator
- Lawyer, educator, politician, and civil rights leader
- Loud, commanding voice
- Cut paper collage illustrations

Cline-Ransome, Lesa. *Before She Was Harriet.* (2017)
- James Ransome, illustrator
- Harriet was a spirited slave, Union spy, she led hundreds to freedom on the Underground Railroad
- Stunning watercolors
- Junior Library Guild Selection
- Coretta Scott King Honor Book
- Christopher Award winner
- Jane Addams Children's Honor Book

Pimentel, Annette Bay. *Girl Running: Bobbi Gibb and the Boston Marathon.* (2018)
- Micha Archer, illustrator
- First woman to run the Boston Marathon in 1966
- Vivid collage illustrations with tissue paper and hand-stamped patterned papers

Ahmed, Roda. *Mae Among the Stars.* (2018)
- Stacia Burrington, illustrator
- The first African American woman to travel in space
- She had incredible success working at NASA
- Playful paintings

Lang, Heather. *Anybody's Game: Kathryn Johnston, the First Girl to Play Little League Baseball.* (2018)
- Cecilia Puglesi, illustrator

- In 1950 girls couldn't play Little League baseball
- Katheryn had the skills so she cut her hair and tried out as "Tubby" and made the team
- There was actually a legal fight to allow girls to play
- Digital illustrations

Engle, Margarita. *The Flying Girl: How Aida de Acosta Learned to Soar.* (2018)
- Sara Palacias, illustrator
- True biography of the first woman to fly a motorized aircraft
- She had courage and the desire to fly – all she needed was a chance
- Bright, colorful, full-page illustrations

Smith, Matthew Clark. *Lighter than Air: Sophie Blanchard, the First Woman Pilot.* (2017)
- Matt Travares, illustrator
- Sophie Blanchard (1778–1819) claimed to be the very first female pilot in France
- Illustrated in ink and watercolor

Stone, Tanya Lee. *Who Says Women Can't Be Computer Programmers? The Story of Ada Lovelace.* (2018)
- Marjorie Priceman, illustrator
- Biography of the first computer programmer
- Daughter of internationally acclaimed poet Lord Byron
- She wrote sophisticated notes on Charles Babbage's Analytical Engine
- Gouache-and-ink artwork complete with numbers, letters, and mathematical symbols

Weatherford, Carole Boston. *Dorothea Lange: The Photographer Who Found the Faces of the Depression.* (2017)
- Sarah Green, illustrator
- Biography of Dorothea Lange – the photographer of the Great Depression
- Her subjects - the downtrodden – the homeless, former slaves, and past executives standing in soup lines
- She had a limp from a bout with polio and felt for the less fortunate
- Digitally painted photos have a 1930s look

Maclear, Kyo. *Bloom: A Story of Fashion Designer Elsa Schiaparelli.* (2018)
- Julie Morstad, illustrator
- Biography of a young girl in Rome who felt ugly and started early on a search for beauty
- In the 1920s and 30s she created unusual fashion designs in Paris
- Hats shaped like shoes, a dress adorned with lobsters, gloves with fingernails, a dress with drawers, etc.
- Vivid mixed-media illustrations

HISTORY

Hopkinson, Deborah. *Ordinary, Extraordinary Jane Austen: The Story of Six Novels, Three Notebooks, a Writing Box, and One Clever Girl.* (2018)
- Qin Leng, illustrator
- Biography of beloved writer, Jane Austen
- A quiet child who loved to read and read everything and then eventually began writing her own stories
- She had a new way of storytelling: "to hold up a mirror to the ordinary world so readers could recognize (and laugh at) themselves"
- The 19th century was difficult for a woman to be an author
- Gentle ink and watercolor illustrations

Krull, Kathleen. *No Truth Without Ruth: The Life of Ruth Bader Ginsburg.* (2018)
- Nancy Zhang, illustrator
- Biography of the second female Supreme Court Justice
- Throughout college, law school, and her work life, she had to face discrimination for being a woman
- She was a warrior for equality, defender of justice, and a trailblazer for girls everywhere
- Large, colorful illustrations

Levy, Debbie. *I Dissent: Ruth Bader Ginsburg Makes Her Mark.* (2016)
- Elizabeth Baddeley, illustrator
- Disagreeing does not make you disagreeable
- Story of the Notorious RBG who disagreed with inequality and unfair treatment
- Richly illustrated with cartoon-like drawings

Rappaport, Doreen. *Ruth Objects: The Life of Ruth Bader Ginsburg.* (2020)
- Eric Velasquez, illustrator
- Top-ranked graduate of Cornell and Columbia Law
- Faced discrimination in the field of law for being a female and a Jew
- A cultural icon – she has championed equal pay and opportunity
- She has an amazing mind, she delivers riveting arguments, and she demonstrates a commitment to truth and justice
- Part of the Big Words series
- Dynamic illustrations

Slade, Suzanne. *Dangerous Jane: The Life and Times of Jane Addams, Crusader for Peace.* (2017)
- Alice Ratterree, illustrator
- Her work for peace won her a Nobel Peace Prize
- She established the Hull House in Chicago that provided help and housing

- She exemplified the value of doing what is right regardless of the criticism
- Pale, washed-out watercolor illustrations
- 2018 Bank Street College of Education Best Books of the Year
- 2018 Children's Book Council Notable Social Studies Trade Books for Young People

Maslo, Lina. *Free as a Bird: The Story of Malala.* (2018)
- Story of Malala Yousafzai, human rights activist and the youngest ever winner of the Nobel Peace Prize
- In Pakistan, some believed girls should not be educated - she secretly went to school and spoke up for education in her country
- An enemy tried to silence her voice but she traveled around the world speaking to anyone who would listen – promoting education for all
- Brightly colored large illustrations

Yousafzai, Malala. *Malala's Magic Pencil.* (2017)
- Malala's story told for younger children
- A story of encouragement, finding one's voice, and seeking justice
- Sparse pen and ink outlines with bright, soft watercolor illustrations

Hood, Susan. *Shaking Things Up: 14 Young Women Who Changed the World.* (2018)
- Sophie Blackall, Emily Winfield Martin, Shadra Strickland, Melissa Sweet, LeUyen Pham, Oge Mora, Julie Morstad, Lisa Brown, Selina Alko, Hadley Hooper, Isabel Roxas, Erin Robinson, Sara Palacios, illustrators
- Introduces 14 notable women in history with a full-page illustration and a poem
- 2019 Bank Street Best Book of the Year
- 2019 Texas Topaz Nonfiction Reading List
- Cooperative Children's Book Center Choices Book 2019
- Notable Social Studies Trade Books for Young People 2019
- Cuyahoga County Public Library's 2018 list of Great Books for Kids

Harrison, Vashti. *Little Leaders: Bold Women in Black History.* (2017)
- Stories of 40 black women trailblazers in history
- They may be little but they accomplished amazing things
- Full-page colorful illustrations
- New York Times Bestseller
- USA Today Bestseller

Rappaport, Doreen. *Elizabeth Started All the Trouble.* (2016)
- Matt Faulkner, illustrator
- One of the first champions for women's rights – Elizabeth Cady Stanton

- The whole crusade took 75 years – but she was at the beginning of the fight
- Colorful illustrations

Van Allsburg, Chris. *Queen of the Falls.* (2011)
- About a 62-year-old woman – the first to go over Niagara Falls in a barrel
- Framed illustrations appear like old-time photos

Clinton, Chelsea. *She Persisted Around the World: 13 Women Who Changed History.* (2018)
- Alexandra Boiger, illustrator
- A companion book to the one specifically about American notable women
- Featuring women from all over the world who overcame many obstacles to follow their dreams
- Watercolor and ink illustrations

Adler, David A. *A Picture Book of Amelia Earhart.* (1999)
- Jeff Fisher, illustrator
- In 1937 this pioneering woman pilot was trying to fly around the globe when she disappeared
- Best remembered as an aviator, she played football and studied auto-repair
- Realistic, double-page watercolor illustrations

Harness, Cheryl. *Mary Walker Wears the Pants: The True Story of the Doctor, Reformer, and Civil War Hero.* (2013)
- Carlo Molinari, illustrator
- An unconventional woman – one of the first women doctors, a suffragist, and she wore pants
- She served in the fields as a commissioned doctor in a modified Union Army uniform
- The first woman to receive the Medal of Honor
- Full-page illustrations in browns and dark blues

WAR

Brown, Don. *Henry and the Cannons: An Extraordinary True Story of the American Revolution.* (2013)
- True story of how Henry Knox dragged 59 cannons from Fort Ticonderoga, New York to Boston
- He moved 120,000 pounds of artillery in winter
- Washington desperately needed the cannons to fight the Revolutionary War
- Watercolor illustrations

Bunting, Eve. *The Wall.* (2015)
- Ronald Himler, illustrator
- A young boy and his dad travel to the Vietnam Veterans' Memorial Wall in Washington, D.C.
- They find the grandfather's name
- Gauzy watercolor illustrations

Walsh, Barbara. *The Poppy Lady: Moina Bell Michael and Her Tribute to Veterans.* (2012)
- Layne Johnson, illustrator
- During World War I Moina established the red poppy as a symbol to honor and remember soldiers
- Even today the red poppy is a symbol for veterans
- Oil paintings
- A portion of the book's proceeds will support the National Military Family Association's Operation Purple®, which benefits children of the U.S. military

Rockwell, Anne. *They Called Her Molly Pitcher.* (2002)
- Cynthia von Buhler, illustrator
- The true story of an American Revolution heroine
- In 1777, Washington made Molly a sergeant in the Continental Army
- She went along with the troops on the battlefield to bring them pitchers of water
- She even fired the cannon when her husband was injured
- Illustrations - folk-art style, sturdy brushwork, light crackling effects = a colonial look

Kodama, Tatsuharu. *Shin's Tricycle.* (1995)
- Noriyuki Ando, illustrator
- True story of a family's experiences when the bomb was dropped in Hiroshima
- Shin is found in the rubble holding on to his tricycle
- He dies later that day – he is not yet four years old – disturbing story
- The tricycle sits in the Peace Museum in Hiroshima
- Somber oil paintings

Winter, Jonah. *The Secret Project.* (2017)
- Jeanette Winter, illustrator
- A boys' school in the remote desert of New Mexico is taken over by the government
- The world's greatest scientists assemble for - The Manhattan Project
- They are sworn to secrecy and there is maximum security as they develop the atomic bomb
- Acrylic and pen illustrations

Maruki, Toshi. *Hiroshima No Pika.* (1980)
- A true story of human suffering brought about by the atomic bomb in Hiroshima
- Told by a small child – what happens to the family after the bomb went off
- Illustrations are haunting and disturbing
- Ehon Nippon Prize - most excellent picture book of Japan

HISTORY

Myers, Walter Dean. *Patrol: An American Soldier in Vietnam.* (2005)
- Ann Grifalconi, illustrator
- The author joined the army on his 17th birthday
- A day in the life of a combat soldier on patrol in Vietnam
- Collage illustrations

Barker, Michelle. *A Year of Borrowed Men.* (2016)
- Renne Benoit, illustrator
- Based on a true story that took place in Germany during World War II and told by a 7-year old girl
- Three French prisoners of war are sent to work on a family farm
- The family is threatened with harm if they help or befriend the prisoners in any way
- They do anyway
- Watercolor and colored pencil illustrations
- 2016 Toronto Dominion Canadian Children's Literature Award shortlist
- 2017 Golden Oak Award shortlist
- 2017 Chocolate Lily Book Award shortlist
- 2016 Canadian Children's Book Centre *Best Books for Kids & Teens* selection

Fleming, Candace. *Boxes for Katje.* (2003)
- Stacey Dressen-McQueen, illustrator
- Post-World War II – Olst, Holland
- Postman brings Katje and her family a care package from America
- Begins an exchange between Katje's townspeople and friends in the USA
- Excellent story of helping and caring
- Colored pencil, oil pastel, and acrylic illustrations, with historical details
- 2004 Bank Street - Best Children's Book of the Year
- 2006 California Young Readers Medal for Picture Books for Older Readers

Tonatiuh, Duncan. *Soldier for Equality: José de la Luz Sáenz and the Great War.* (2019)
- Luz was born in the US but often discriminated against for his Mexican heritage
- He served in WWI as a valuable member of the intelligence office in Europe because he could quickly learn different languages
- Still discriminated against – came home to start the League of United Latin American Citizens – the largest and oldest Latinx civil rights organization
- Pre-Columbian inspired illustrations
- Orbis Pictus Honor Book Award for Outstanding Nonfiction for Children 2020
- 2020 Pura Belpré Author Honor Book
- Robert F. Sibert Medal

Hopkinson, Deborah. *Knit Your Bit: A World War I Story.* (2013)
- Steven Guarnaccia, illustrator
- Based on a real "knit-in" event at Central Park in 1918
- Girls challenging boys to do their part to knit clothes for soldiers during WW1
- Pen and ink and watercolor illustrations

Greenwood, Mark. *Midnight: A True Story of Loyalty in World War I.* (2015)
- Frane Lessac, illustrator
- True, sad tale of a World War I cavalry soldier and his heroic horse, Midnight
- Bright and colorful gouache paintings

Smith, Icy. *Half Spoon of Rice: A Survival Story of Cambodian Genocide.* (2010)
- Sopaul Nhem, illustrator
- True story of Nat and his family's struggles during the Cambodian Genocide, 1975-79
- Nat endures four years of separation from his family, starvation, and brutality
- Bold, impressionistic oil illustrations, and historical photographs
- Benjamin Franklin Silver Award
- California Book Award Finalist
- Society of School Librarians International Honor Award
- Cooperative Children Book Center Choices Skipping Stones Honor Award
- Moonbeam Children's Book Award

Polacco, Patricia. *Pink and Say.* (1994)
- Story set during the Civil War
- Say, who is white and wounded, is nursed back to health by a black soldier's family
- The story has a very sad ending
- Heartbreaking illustrations

Rumford, James. *Silent Music: A Story of Baghdad.* (2008)
- Ali, a young boy in Baghdad, turns to writing when bombs are falling outside all around
- Collage, pencil and charcoal illustrations and calligraphy
- 2009 Bank Street - Best Children's Book of the Year.

Sís, Peter. *The Wall: Growing Up Behind the Iron Curtain.* (2007)
- Autobiography of the author who grew up in Prague, Czechoslovakia under Soviet rule
- Tells of secret police – they intrude on every page
- Definitely for middle/high school students
- Sparing use of color – black, white, and Communist red
- 2007 New York Times Book Review Best Illustrated Book of the Year

- 2008 Caldecott Honor Book
- 2008 Bank Street - Best Children's Book of the Year
- 2008 Boston Globe - Horn Book Award for Nonfiction
- 2008 Eisner Award for Best Publication for Kids

Demarest, Chris L. *Alpha Bravo Charlie: The Military Alphabet.* (2005)
- Details about the International Communications Alphabet
- The military uses a word for each letter of the alphabet for clarity and continuity
- The US Navy also has color coded flags for each letter
- Brightly colored pastel illustrations

Heide, Florence Parry. *Sami and the Time of Troubles.* (1992)
- Judith Heide Gilliland, illustrator
- A young boy wishes for peace in his war-torn city of Beirut
- Watercolor illustrations

GOVERNMENT

Main characters are mice and often the focus is cheese but these stories relate the basic operations of the government in a light-hearted but informative way.

Cheryl Shaw Barnes, illustrator

Barnes, Peter W. *House Mouse, Senate Mouse.* (2012)
Barnes, Peter W. *Marshall, The Courthouse Mouse: A Tail of the U.S. Supreme Court.* (2012)
Barnes, Peter W. *Woodrow, The White House Mouse.* (2012)
Barnes, Peter W. *Woodrow for President: A Tail of Voting, Campaigns, and Elections.* (2012)
Barnes, Peter W. *Liberty Lee's Tail of Independence.* (2012)

ANCIENT HISTORY

Ancient China

Noyes, Deborah. *Red Butterfly: How a Princess Smuggled the Secret of Silk Out of China.* (2007)
- Sophie Blackall, illustrator
- Tale about a princess betrothed to someone in a foreign land
- Her connection to her homeland via the silk worm is the point of the story
- Light pastel colors and fine line illustrations

Major, John. *The Silk Route: 7,000 Miles of History.* (1995)
- Stephen Fieser, illustrator
- Informative work on the commerce, culture, and trade along the silk road
- Pair with the "Red Butterfly" a tale about the value/treasure that was the silkworm
- Lavish, full-page illustrations

Christensen, Bonnie. *A Single Pebble: The Story of the Silk Road.* (2013)
- Setting in 9th century China
- Traveling the silk road all the way to the end
- Provides glimpses of different cultures along the way
- Colorful illustrations and maps

Ancient Egypt

Bunting, Eve. *I Am the Mummy Heb-Nefert.* (1997)
- David Christiana, illustrator
- For older readers
- About the life of an Egyptian royal who died and became a mummy
- She looks back on her privileged life
- Hauntingly beautiful watercolor illustrations

Sabuda, Robert. *Tutankhamen's Gift.* (1997)
- About the reign of Amenhotep and his efforts to unify the gods by destroying temples
- After his mysterious death Tutankhamen takes over
- Great discussion starter on the value of art and culture
- Brilliant and colorful illustrations
- New York Times Notable Children's Book

Abouraya, Karen Leggett. *Hands Around the Library: Protecting Egypt's Treasured Books.* (2011)
- Susan L. Roth, illustrator
- True story – January 2011 – a demonstration to protect the Library of Alexandria in Egypt
- Beautiful collage illustrations

Rumford, James. *Seeker of Knowledge: The Man Who Deciphered Egyptian Hieroglyphs.* (2000)
- Biography of Jean-Francois Champollion, 19th century scholar who first deciphered hieroglyphics
- Beautiful watercolor illustrations, with soft blues, purples, and sunlit pinks

Aliki. *Mummies Made in Egypt.* (1985)
- Excellent introduction to Ancient Egypt's gods and mummies
- Colorful and informative illustrations

HISTORY

Andronik, Catherine M. *Hatshepsut, His Majesty, Herself.* (2001)
- Joseph Daniel Fiedler, illustrator
- Biography of Hatshepsut, the only female pharaoh who used a male title and wore men's clothing and a beard
- Her nephew tried to erase all traces of her very successful reign but archaeologists prevailed to tell her story
- Beautiful illustrations and maps

Trumble, Kelly. *Cat Mummies.* (1998)
- Laszlo Kubinyi, illustrator
- Answers the question of why Egyptians mummified thousands and thousands of cats
- Tells why/how Egyptians lost a war with Persians in 542 BC because of cats
- The book offers a chronology of Egyptian history
- Soft-focus watercolor illustrations

Frank, John. *The Tomb of the Boy King: A True Story in Verse.* (2001)
- Tom Pohrt, illustrator
- An epic poem about the discovery of King Tut's tomb
- Blend of alliteration and imagery
- Noted as superb read-aloud for older students
- Graceful watercolors and muted sepia toned illustrations recall old photographs and borders filled with hieroglyphs and Egyptian motifs

Love, D. Anne. *Of Numbers and Stars: The Story of Hypatia.* (2006)
- Pam Paparone, illustrator
- Biography of Hypatia, an Egyptian woman who lived in 4th century Alexandria
- Women were not educated then but her father insisted
- She became a respected scholar in mathematics and philosophy
- Illustrations with Egyptian motifs

ANCIENT GREECE

Usher, M.D. *Wise Guy: The Life and Philosophy of Socrates.* (2005)
- William Bramhall, illustrator
- Good, straightforward introduction to Socrates
- His ideas about wisdom, right and wrong, courage, justice, and love
- His method of thinking did not sit well with everyone - fellow Athenians punished him with death
- For older students
- Ink and watercolor illustrations

Ancient India

Whelan, Gloria. *In Andal's House.* (2013)
- Amanda Hall, illustrator
- An introduction to the Hindu caste system
- Vibrant and colorful illustrations

Ancient Islam

Demi. *Muhammad.* (2003)
- He was born into a powerful and influential Meccan tribe in the year AD 570
- Reflects the literary and artistic traditions of the Islamic world
- A clear overview of Islam
- Beautiful paint and ink illustrations

Barnard, Bryn. *The Genius of Islam: How Muslims Made the Modern World.* (2011)
- Our numbers are a Muslim invention
- Marching bands started in the Middle East
- Modern cities have roots in Islamic architecture
- Muslim contributions are featured in this picture book
- Full color illustrations

Kahn, Hena. *Golden Domes and Silver Lanterns: A Muslim Book of Colors.* (2012)
- Mehrdokht Amini, illustrator
- Simple text in rhyme
- Great information about the Muslim culture
- Beautiful illustrations

Cunnane, Kelly. *Deep in the Sahara.* (2013)
- Hoda Hadadi, illustrator
- Authentic Islamic cultural details
- Poetic language and beautiful illustrations

Ancient Japan

Spivak, Dawnine. *Grass Sandals: The Travels of Basho.* (1997)
- Demi, illustrator
- Basho is a great Japanese haiku poet (1644-1694)
- Many of his haiku poems are included
- Typical Japanese artwork and Japanese characters

HISTORY

Ray, Deborah Kogan. *Hokusai: The Man Who Painted a Mountain.* (2001)
- A famous and influential Japanese artist known for painting Mt. Fuji (1760-1849)
- Painted a lion-dog daily for good luck
- Wealthy would not buy his art because he was a peasant
- Wash and colored pencil illustrations

ANCIENT WEST AFRICA

Maddern, Eric. *The Fire Children: A West African Folktale.* (2015)
- Frane Lessac, illustrator
- A West African creation story
- West African masks and pottery
- Illustrations are brightly colored gouache paintings

Wisniewski, David. *Sundiata: Lion King of Mali.* (1992)
- Combination of biography and legend
- A 13th century prince – a social outcast with physical handicaps, triumphs over strong opposition to become the ruler of Mali
- Brightly colored cut paper collage illustrations

A monthly update, with many reviewed, additional titles, will be available to you if you email me at brainfitness78@gmail.com Log on to www.cognitive-fitness.com to see my other work.
-

Language Arts

LANGUAGE ARTS

Herrera, Juan Felipe. *Imagine.* (2018)
- Lauren Castilla, illustrator
- Story of the young boy who became the U. S, Poet Laureate
- Warm, deftly composed illustrations, with the sensual allure of woodcuts

Wimmer, Sonja. *The Word Collector.* (2012)
- Haunting descriptions of words and the power they hold - make this a favorite for linguaphiles
- Great message about kindness
- Text is sometimes difficult to read – but it is all, clearly printed at the end
- The text is incorporated into the delightful collage illustrations
- 2011 Moonbeam Children's Book Awards

Maurer, Tracy Nelson. *Noah Webster's Fighting Words.* (2017)
- Mircea Catusonu, illustrator
- Born in 1758, Webster was a young Yale student during the Revolutionary War
- He used his words as weapons to fight against British cultural dominance
- He had bold ideas and strong opinions about everything
- Mixed media and collage illustrations

Alexander, Kwame, Chris Colderley and Marjorie Wentworth. *Out of Wonder: Poems Celebrating Poets.* (2017)
- Ekua Holmes, illustrator
- A collection of verse that pays homage to 20 notable poets
- Celebrating poets with original verse is an excellent prompt for creative writing
- Mixed media and layered collage illustrations
- 2018 Coretta Scott King Illustrator Award Winner
- New York Times Best Seller

Truss, Lynne. *Eats, Shoots & Leaves: Why, Commas Really Do Make a Difference!* (2006)
- Bonnie Timmons, illustrator
- Each two-page spread shows a sentence with incorrect and correct comma usage
- Ink and water color illustrations

Sutcliffe, Jane. *Will's Words: How William Shakespeare Changed the Way You Talk.* (2016)
- John Shelley, illustrator
- Find out exactly how Shakespeare changed the English language forever
- The story of the words and phrases that Shakespeare brought to the English language
- Background information on the Globe Theater and London during Shakespeare's time
- Double page illustrations crowded with intricate, colorful details

Stanley, Diane. *The Bard of Avon: The Story of William Shakespeare.* (2015)
- Peter Vennema, illustrator
- Shakespeare, with a grade school education, grew to be the most famous English-speaking playwright in the world
- Since Ancient Greece – drama had died out until Elizabethan London when plays were finally performed again in many theaters
- There were playwrights and companies of actors where Shakespeare was considered to be a man for all time
- Distinctive full-color gouache illustrations

GRAMMAR

A collection of picture books on parts of speech with brightly colored, amazing illustrations as well as great vocabulary and lessons for learning and reviewing parts of speech – definitely worth looking into! Artwork suitable for framing.

Heller, Ruth. *A Cache of Jewels and Other Collective Nouns.* (1998)
Heller, Ruth. *Kites Sail High: A Book About Verbs.* (1998)
Heller, Ruth. *Mine, All Mine!: A Book About Pronouns.* (1999)
Heller, Ruth. *Merry-Go-Round: A Book About Nouns.* (1998)
Heller, Ruth. *Up Up and Away: A Book About Adverbs.* (1998)
Heller, Ruth. *Many Luscious Lollipops: A Book About Adjectives.* (1998)
Heller, Ruth. *Behind the Mask: A Book About Prepositions.* (1998)
Heller, Ruth. *Fantastic! Wow! And Unreal! A Book About Interjections and Conjunctions.* (2000)

CINDERELLA STORIES

The Cinderella story is known around the world. Here are most of them retold through the lens of a specific culture. Great for creative writing and cultural studies. Illustrations are fitting and beautiful.

Ai-Ling Louie. *Yeh Shen: A Cinderella Story from China.* (1996)
- Ed Young, illustrator

Climo, Shirley. *The Egyptian Cinderella.* (1992)
- Ruth Heller, illustrator

Manna, Anthony and Christodoula Mitakidou. *The Orphan: A Cinderella Story from Greece.* (2011)
- Giselle Potter, illustrator

Hickox, Rebecca. *The Golden Sandal: A Middle Eastern Cinderella Story.* (1999)
- Will Hillenbrand, illustrator

Climo, Shirley. *The Korean Cinderella.* (1996)
- Ruth Heller, illustrator

Lowell, Susan. *Cindy Ellen: A Wild Western Cinderella.* (2001)
- Jane Manning, illustrator

Climo, Shirley. *The Persian Cinderella.* (2001)
- Robert Florczak, illustrator

Dwyer, Mindy. *The Salmon Princess: An Alaskan Cinderella.* (2004)

San Souci, Robert. *Cendrillon: A Caribbean Cinderella.* (2002)
- Brian Pickney, illustrator

Martin, Rafe. *The Rough-Face Girl: An Algonquin Indian Tale.* (1998)
- David Shannon, illustrator

Climo, Shirley. *The Irish Cinderlad.* (2000)
- Loretta Krupinski, illustrator

Coburn, Jewell Reinhart. *Angkat: The Cambodian Cinderella.* (2013)
- Eddie Flotte, illustrator

Schroeder, Alan. *Smoky Mountain Rose: An Appalachian Cinderella.* (2000)
- Brad Sneed, illustrator

Bradford, Deborah Denise. *Kangaroo Princess: An Australian Cinderella Story.* (2015)
- James Crumby, illustrator

Pollock, Penny. *The Turkey Girl: A Zuni Cinderella Story.* (1996)
- Ed Young, illustrator

Guarnaccia, Steven. *Cinderella: A Fashionable Tale.* (2013)

Marceau-Chenkie, Brittany. *Naya, An Inuit Cinderella.* (1999)
- Shelley Brookes, illustrator

Sierra, Judy. *The Gift of the Crocodile: A Cinderella Story.* (2000)
- Reynold Ruffins, illustrator

San Souci, Robert D. *Sootface An Ojibway Cinderella Story.* (1997)
- Dabiel San Souci, illustrator

San Souci, Robert D. *Cinderella Skeleton.* (2004)
- David Catrow, illustrator

Perlman, Janet. *Cinderella Penguin, or, The Little Glass Flipper.* (1995)

Johnston, Tony. *Bigfoot Cinderrrrrella.* (2000)
- James Warhola, illustrator

Meddaugh, Susan. *Cinderella's Rat.* (2002)

Coburn, Jewell Reinhart. *Domítíla: A Cinderella Tale from the Mexican Tradition.* (2014)
- Connie McLennan, illustrator

De la Paz, Myrna. *Abadeha: The Philippine Cinderella Cinderella in a Hot Air Balloon.* (2014)
- Youshan Tany, illustrator

dePaola, Tommie. *Adelita, A Mexican Cinderella Story.* (2014)

Shaskan, Trisha Speed and Trisha Sue Speed Shaskan. *Seriously, Cinderella Is SO Annoying!: The Story*

of Cinderella as Told by the Wicked Stepmother (The Other Side of the Story). (2011)
- Gerald Claude Guerlais, illustrator

Auch, Mary Jane. *Chickerella.* (2005)
- Herm Auch, illustrator

Underwood, Deborah. *Interstellar Cinderella.* (2015)
- Meg Hunt, illustrator

CREATIVE WRITING IDEAS

Lehman, Barbara. *Museum Trip.* (2006) WORDLESS
- Class visit to the museum and what happens if a student becomes part of an exhibit
- There's a blurry line between reality and imagination
- Watercolor, gouache, and ink illustrations

Wisniewski, David. *Tough Cookie.* (1999)
- A hilarious spoof about the adventures of a private eye
- Cut paper illustrations shaded with colored pencils

Yamada, Kobi. *What Do You Do With an Idea?* (2014)
- Mae Besom, illustrator
- The development of an idea through the eyes of a child
- Muted color illustrations
- *Wall Street Journal Best Seller*
- *USA Today Best Seller*
- *Publishers Weekly Best Seller*
- New York Times Best Seller
- Independent Publishers Award
- Washington State Book Award
- Moonbeam Children's Book Award.

Robinson, Christian. *Another.* (2019) WORDLESS
- Is there another someone out there in another universe who is exactly like you?
- Brightly colored illustrations against a stark white background
- National Public Radio Favorite Book of 2019
- New York Times Best Children's Book of 2019
- New York Public Library Best Book of 2019
- Publishers Weekly Best Book of 2019
- School Library Journal Best Picture Book of 2019
- BookPage Best Picture Book of 2019
- Horn Book Fanfare Selection of 2019

Munsch, Robert. *Paperbag Princess.* (1980)
- Michael Martchenko, illustrator
- A classic story of girl power – with the best ending line – EVER!
- A fierce dragon burns down Elizabeth's castle and kidnaps her fiancé – Prince Ronald
- Elizabeth, with only a paper bag to wear, chases down the dragon and gives him what for and saves Prince Ronald
- Watercolor and ink illustrations

Coelho, Rogerio. *Boat of Dreams.* (2017) WORDLESS
- A story of an old man who lives by the sea and finds a bottle with a paper inside
- He draws a ship on the paper and returns it to the bottle and the sea
- The story is a starting point for imaginative developments according to each individual reader
- Sepia illustrations
- 2018 Bank Street College of Education Best Children's Books of the Year
- 2017 New York Public Library Best Books for Kids List
- 2017 Independent Book Publisher Awards (IPPY) Gold Medalist
- Brazil's 2015 Jabuti Award for Best Children's Illustration

Ellis, Carson. *Du Iz Tak?* (2016)
- Almost wordless with only alienlike, invented dialogue
- Setting is a small piece of ground where several insects reside
- The story unfolds through the passing of the seasons
- Illustrations with exquisite detail
- 2017 Caldecott Honor Book
- EB White Read-Aloud Award

Santat, Dan. *After the Fall* (*How Humpty Dumpty Got Back Up Again*) (2017)
- An important message – life begins when you get back up
- After the fall Humpty is afraid of heights and can't do many of the things he likes
- Triumphant ending
- Colorful illustrations
- 2018 National Council of Teachers of English Charlotte Huck Award Winner
- Kirkus Reviews Best Picture Book of 2017
- New York Times Notable Children's Book of 2017
- New York City Public Library Notable Best Book for Kids
- Chicago Public Library Best Book of 2017
- Horn Book Fanfare Best Book of 2017
- National Public Radio Best Book of 2017

Klassen, Jon. *I Want My Hat Back.* (2011)
- A great example of a repetitive tale – a formula with a twist
- A subtle endorsement of murder
- Browns and a splash of red illustrations
- New York Times Best Illustrated Children's Book of 2011

Morris, Richard T. *This is a Moose.* (2014)
- Tom Lichtenfeld, illustrator
- A movie director wants to do a film on the life of a moose
- The starring moose really wants to be an astronaut and go to the moon
- Ink, colored pencil, and gouache illustrations

Willems, Mo. *That Is Not a Good Idea!* (2013)
- A young fox invites a plump duck to dinner in true evil villain – innocent damsel style
- Presented in silent movie format – with a bunch of chicks in the audience repeating that - this is not a good idea
- Colorful, full-page illustrations

Sierra, Judy. *Tell the Truth, B. B. Wolf.* (2010)
- J. Otto Seibold, illustrator
- A fractured fairy tale – the "reformed" wolf tells a new version of the tale
- Computer illustrations with comic touches

Wiesner, David. *June 29, 1999.* (1992)
- A totally imaginative tale with wild and delightful illustrations
- A vegetable experience of huge proportions
- Great story and discussion starter
- Watercolor illustrations - stark and realistic
- 1993 American Library Association Notable Book
- School Library Journal Best Books of 1992
- Horn Book's Outstanding Books of the Year 1993
- Publishers Weekly 50 Best Books of 1992
- New York Times Notable Books of the Year 1992

Wiesner, David. *Flotsam.* (2006)
- A boy walks on the beach examining the flotsam
- What he finds is quite amazing
- A wide variety of story and discussion starters within the story
- Vivid, realistic watercolor illustrations
- Caldecott Medal 2007

Wiesner, David. *Tuesday.* (1991)
- Fat frogs riding lily pads over a swamp on a Tuesday evening at eight
- Eventually flying over the countryside and town and causing all kinds of surprises
- Watercolor illustrations
- Caldecott Medal 1992
- American Library Association Notable Children's Book

Wiesner, David. *Sector 7.* (1999) WORDLESS
- The story begins with a school trip to the Empire State Building – at the top – total cloud cover
- A boy is whisked away on a cloud to the Cloud Dispatch Center for Sector 7 which is New York City
- There the adventure begins
- Watercolor illustrations with fine line details
- Caldecott Honor 2000

Wiesner, David. *Hurricane.* (1990)
- Two brothers are safe and warm in their home as a hurricane passes
- A giant elm tree falls in their yard and it becomes the pathway for exciting imaginary adventures
- Watercolor illustrations

Wiesner, David. *Free Fall.* (2008) WORDLESS
- Boy falls asleep with a book in his arms
- Dreams all sorts of exciting events – amazing illustrations
- Caldecott Honor 1989
- American Library Association Notable Children's Book

Wiesner, David. *The Three Pigs.* (2001)
- Minimal text – beginning the traditional three pigs' story
- Then off the page illustrations and a far-out story line
- Dialog balloons and a wide variety of illustration styles
- Caldecott Medal 2002

Tan, Shaun. *Rules of Summer.* (2014)
- About the rules imposed on a younger sibling by his older brother
- Older students – possibly examples of context clues and prediction
- Strange but unique story
- Vibrant full-page illustrations

Barnett, Mac. *Sam & Dave Dig a Hole.* (2014)
- Jon Klassen, illustrator
- Two boys dig a hole in the hopes of finding something spectacular
- Only the reader can see that every time they change directions, they just miss something spectacular
- Mixed-media, muted earth tones, uncomplicated illustrations
- 2015 Caldecott Honor Book
- Irma S and James H Black Award for Excellence in Children's Literature

Cummins, Lucy Ruth. *A Hungry Lion or A Dwindling Assortment of Animals.* (2016)
- The hungry lion begins the day with a large assortment of animal friends
- As the day progresses, the animals start to disappear
- What is happening to the animals?
- Adorable, scribbly illustrations

Fleischman, Paul. *The Dunderheads.* (2009)
- David Roberts, illustrator
- Miss Breakbone hates kids - especially the troublesome students in her class
- However – the dunderheads end up teaching her a lesson
- Quirky, hilarious illustrations with pen and ink and splashes of color

Hurston, Zora Neale and Joyce Carol Thomas. *Lies and Other Tall Tales.* (2005)
- Christopher Myers, illustrator
- A collection of VERY far-fetched tales gathered while traveling the south in the early 1900s
- Bold and wildly expressive collage illustrations

Macaulay, David. *Black and White.* (1990)
- Four stories in black and white told in four quadrants across double pages
- Is this a story? A Puzzle? A game? Or what?
- Colorful illustrations

Myers, Christopher. *H.O.R.S.E.: A Game of Basketball and Imagination.* (2012)
- Two kids play a game of H.O.R.S.E. on an urban basketball court
- Their shots are wildly creative, imaginative, and quite astounding
- Combination of gouache and art paper collage illustrations

Rodriguez, Béatrice. *The Chicken Thief.* (2010) WORDLESS
- Lesson is – how things appear is not always how they really are
- Pen and ink and watercolor illustrations

Rosenthal, Amy Krouse. *Exclamation Mark.* (2013)
- Tom Lichtenheld, illustrator
- A story of the most exuberant punctuation mark of all
- Spare, clever, black-outlined punctuation marks with faces on kindergarten-style writing paper

Smith, Lane. *It's a Book.* (2010)
- The characters: a mouse, a donkey, and a monkey are examining a book
- Raised in the digital age – one character does not know quite how to operate a book
- Full page, stylized illustrations provide a great backdrop

Wenzel, Brendan. *They All Saw a Cat.* (2016)
- A celebration of observation, curiosity, and imagination
- Amazing, colorful illustrations
- New York Times Bestseller of 2016 and 2017
- School Library Journal Best Book of 2016
- Junior Library Guild Selection of 2016
- American Booksellers Council 2016 Best Books for Children
- 2016 Amazon Best Book of the Month

Willis, Jeanne. *Tadpole's Promise.* (2005)
- Tony Ross, illustrator
- A tongue-in-cheek love story
- A tadpole and a caterpillar fall in love and promise they will never change
- Of course, that's not possible and perhaps you can guess the ending?
- Vibrantly hued pen and ink and watercolor illustrations

Hartman, Bob. *The Wolf Who Cried Boy.* (2002)
- Tim Raglin, illustrator
- A well-written, hilarious twist on the original story
- Sturdy pen and ink illustrations

Palatini, Margie. *The Cheese.* (2007)
- Steve Johnson and Lou Fancher, illustrators
- A hilarious, reverse version of the Farmer in the Dell with the rat in charge
- Why should good food go to waste because of a silly song?
- Colorful folk-art illustrations

Scieszka, Jon. *The True Story of the Three Little Pigs.* (1999)
- Lane Smith, illustrator
- A. Wolf tries to set the record straight from the big house

- He was framed!
- Funny retelling of the classic tale from the wolf's point of view
- Highly imaginative illustrations

Scieszka, Jon. *The Stinky Cheese Man and Other Fairly Stupid Tales.* (1992)
- Lane Smith, illustrator
- All the fairy tales you know and love retold in very funny way
- Even the format of the book does not escape hilarious mocking by the storyteller
- Possible ideas for creative rewriting of other stories and tales
- Illustrations with intricate detail work

Willems, Mo. *Goldilocks and the Three Dinosaurs.* (2012)
- A hilarious spoof on the original Goldilocks story
- Embedded jokes for all age levels!
- Many visual gags in the cleanly drawn illustrations

Rex, Adam. *Nothing Rhymes with Orange.* (2017)
- A silly but cute story about how orange feels being left out of poems and rhymes
- But then the fruit parade comes up with a way to include orange
- Good lesson on celebrating differences and inclusiveness
- Bright, colorful, full-page illustrations
- Huffington Post Best Book of the Year
- Chicago Tribune Best Children's Books of the Year

Browne, Anthony. *Voices in the Park.* (2001)
- A visit to the park from multiple perspectives
- Colorful illustrations

A monthly update, with many reviewed, additional titles, will be available to you if you email me at brainfitness78@gmail.com Log on to www.cognitive-fitness.com to see my other work.

The Arts

THE ARTS

Knapp, Ruthie. *Who Stole Mona Lisa?* (2010)
- Jill McElmurry, illustrator
- Whimsical biography of Mona Lisa
- Told from the viewpoint of the painting
- Tells the story of the "kidnapping" from the Louvre
- Rich gouache colors and fancifully adorned illustrations

Steptoe, Javaka. *Radiant Child: The Story of Young Artist Jean-Michel Basquait.* (2016)
- Biography of modern art phenomenon Jean-Michel Basquiat
- Bold artwork and collage-style paintings
- Randolph Caldecott Medal Award 2017
- Coretta Scott King Illustrator Award 2017

Wallace, Sandra Neil. *Between the Lines: How Ernie Barnes Went from the Football Field to the Art Gallery.* (2018)
- Bryan Collier, illustrator
- An artist who played football for the Colts
- When he retired from football, he became the official artist for the American Football League
- Dynamic, mixed media illustrations
- 2019 Orbis Pictus Book Award Winner
- American Library Association/Association for Library Service to Children Notable Children's Book
- Society of Children's Book Writers and Illustrators Golden Kite Honor Book Award
- Booklist Top 10 Biographies for Youth
- Booklist Top 10 Art Books for Youth
- New York Public Library Best Book for Kids
- Chicago Public Library Best of the Best Book

Say, Allen. *Silent Days, Silent Dreams.* (2017)
- Celebrating the artwork of James Castle born two months premature in 1899 in Idaho
- He was deaf, mute, and autistic and never learned to speak, read, write, or use sign language
- However, his artwork hangs in major museums around the world
- Color, monochrome, cartoon, snapshot – a variety of illustrations

Willems, Mo. *Because.* (2019)
- A brilliant story that shows how one piece of music can change so many lives
- Beautiful color illustrations

THE ARTS

Polacco, Patricia. *Mr. Wayne's Masterpiece.* (2014)
- Mr. Wayne's drama class terrifies Trisha who hates speaking in front of an audience
- So, she paints scenery but also learns the lines of the lead
- When the lead moves away – with Mr. Wayne's excellent coaching – Trisha is the star!
- Pencil and marker illustrations

Rosenstock, Barb. *The Noisy Paint Box: The Colors and Sounds of Kandinsky's Abstract Art.* (2014)
- Mary GrandPre, illustrator
- Story of Russian-born Vasily Kandinsky – one of the first painters of abstract art
- Richly colored, large acrylic paint and paper collage illustrations

Daywalt, Drew. *The Day the Crayons Quit.* (2013)
- Oliver Jeffers, illustrator
- A box of crayons goes rogue – they each leave a letter detailing their grievances
- Colorful crayon illustrations
- Amazon's 2013 Best Picture Book of the Year
- Barnes & Noble Best Book of 2013
- Goodreads' 2013 Best Picture Book of the Year
- Winner of the EB White Read-Aloud Award

Andrede, Giles. *Giraffes Can't Dance.* (2001)
- Guy Parker-Rees, illustrator
- Text written in rhyme
- Giraffe can't dance at the annual Jungle Dance and is laughed at by the other animals who can
- He gets help from an unlikely source and soon dances the night away
- Bold, brightly colored illustrations

Luyken, Corinna. *The Book of Mistakes.* (2017)
- About the creative process
- It sometimes begins with a mistake
- Colored pencil, pen and ink illustrations

Novesky, Amy. *Me, Frida.* (2010)
- David Diaz, illustrator
- True story of one of the most celebrated artists of all time
- Frida Kahlo, wife of Diego Rivera – also a famous artist
- Rich color illustrations

Tonatiuh, Duncan. *Funny Bones: Posada and His Day of the Dead Calaveras.* (2015)
- Story telling how the funny skeletons – calaveras – came to be
- Now synonymous with Día de los Muertos - Mexican festival
- Mexican style illustrations
- Robert F. Sibert Informational Book Medal
- Pura Belpré Honor Book
- New York Times Best Illustrated Children's Books of 2015
- International Latino Book Award Finalist

Tonatiuh, Duncan. *Diego Rivera: His World and Ours.* (2011)
- Famous painter of the 20th century
- Painted murals depicting historical events in Mexican culture
- Beautiful illustrations

Wiesner, David. *Art & Max.* (2010)
- Whimsical story of two lizards who take a trip through the world of art
- Interesting look at the way artists create
- Acrylic paints, watercolor, and line illustrations

Winter, Jonah. *Just Behave, Pablo Picasso!.* (2012)
- Kevin Hawkes, illustrator
- Biography of Pablo Picasso - highlighting his energy, enthusiasm, and dedication
- Showing how people hated his work – good for budding artists who get criticized
- Colorful illustrations

Brown, Monica. *Frida Kahlo and Her Animalitos.* (2017)
- John Parra, illustrator
- A biography of one of the world's most influential painters, Mexican artist – Frida Kahlo
- Two monkeys, a parrot, three dogs, two turkeys, an eagle, a black cat, and a fawn were the pets that inspired her art and life
- Vibrant acrylic illustrations - done in a folk-art style
- Pura Belpré Illustrator Honor 2018
- American Library Association Notable Children's Book 2018
- New York Times/New York Public Library Best Illustrated Children's Book of 2017
- Barnes & Noble Best Book of 2017
- Smithsonian Top Ten Best Children's Book of 2017
- Bank Street Best Children's Book of the Year 2018

THE ARTS

MUSIC

Golio, Gary. *Bird & Diz.* (2015)
- Ed Young, illustrator
- The characters are sax player Charlie "Bird" Parker and trumpeter John "Dizzy" Gillespie
- Demonstrates the back-and-forth sounds of bebop
- Colorful illustrations representing the sounds and actions

Greenberg, Jan and Sandra Jordan. *Ballet for Martha: Making Appalachian Spring.* (2010)
- Brian Floca, illustrator
- Making of Appalachian Spring – Martha Graham's most famous performance
- Vivid watercolor illustrations
- Orbis Pictus Award for Outstanding Nonfiction for Children

Mahin, Michael. *Muddy: The Story of Blues Legend Muddy Waters.* (2017)
- Evan Turk, illustrator
- The biography of McKinley Morganfield (1913–83), aka Muddy Waters, an American blues legend
- Born in Mississippi, made his own instrument and music while facing opposition everywhere
- Went to Chicago and helped develop a new kind of jazz-blues and eventually cut an album
- Full-page mixed media illustrations with folk-art images
- Ezra Jack Keats New Illustrator Award - Evan Turk
- Outstanding Nonfiction Book Award, Children's Literature Council, Southern California
- New York Times Best Illustrated Book of 2017
- National Public Radio Best Books of 2017
- New York Public Library's 2017 Best Books for Kids Top 10
- Chicago Public Library's 2017 Best Books for Kids List
- Center for the Study of Multicultural Literature's Best Books List 2017
- "Windows and Mirrors" Selection by the New England Children's Booksellers Association
- Parents' Choice Awards Gold Medal
- California Reading Association Eureka! Nonfiction Children's Book Awards Gold Medal
- Junior Library Guild Selection, Fall 2017

Rusch, Elizabeth. *The Music of Life: Cristofori & the Invention of the Piano.* (2017)
- Marjorie Priceman, illustrator
- Prince Ferdinando de Medici wants his court to become the musical center of Italy
- He brings Cristofori – who makes musical instruments - to Florence
- Cristofori creates the pianoforte, an instrument that can play both loud and soft
- Gouache and ink illustrations with bold strokes

Rockliff, Mara. *Born to Swing: Lil Hardin Armstrong's Life in Jazz.* (2018)
- Michele Wood, illustrator
- Lil Hardin Armstrong got a job playing piano in Chicago's hottest jazz band
- She earned acclaim also as a band leader and composer
- She was the wife of Louis Armstrong
- Thickly painted colorful acrylic illustrations

Tonatiuh, Duncan. *Danza!: Amalia Hernandez and Mexico's Folkloric Ballet.* (2017)
- A celebration of a famous dancer and choreographer and the rich history of dance in Mexico
- She learned the dances from all the regions of Mexico
- She opened her own dance company - El Ballet Folklórico de México
- The company became an international sensation and still tours today
- Digital collage illustrations with bright colors, strong patterns, textures, and forms

Krull, Kathleen and Paul Brewer. *The Beatles Were Fab (and They Were Funny).* (2013)
- Stacy Innerst, illustrator
- A new twist – this is about the Beatles' sense of humor
- Lots of information about their fan culture
- Many songs, concert dates, and crazy details are included, even a time line
- Expressive, quirky illustrations

Myers, Walter Dean. *Jazz.* (2006)
- Christopher Myers, illustrator
- Fifteen poems with amazing wordplay and rhythm
- A journey celebrating jazz from its beginnings to present day
- Black-inked acetate over brilliant saturated acrylic illustrations
- Coretta Scott King Award Honor Book
- American Library Association Notable Children's Book
- Lee Bennett Hopkins Poetry Award
- Publishers Weekly's 100 Best Books of the Year
- Kirkus Reviews Editor's Choice
- Booklist Editor's Choice
- Booklist Top Ten in Black History
- Book Link's Best New Books for the Classroom
- Golden Kite Award: Picture Book Text

Neri, G. *Hello, I'm Johnny Cash.* (2014)
- A. G. Ford, illustrator
- Biography – from early life of poverty and challenges
- Elegant introduction
- Illustrations done in oils

Raschka, Chris. *The Cosmobiography of Sun Ra: The Sound of Joy Is Enlightening.* (2014)
- Celebrating the centennial of the birth of jazz musician Sun Ra (1914–1993)
- Outstanding illustrations

Potter, Alicia. *Jubilee: One Man's Big Bold and Very Very Loud Celebration of Peace.* (2014)
- Matt Tavares, illustrator
- The 1869 National Peace Jubilee, the largest and loudest concert the world had ever seen — or heard
- Patrick Sarsfield Gilmore, a band leader in Boston – celebrating the end of the Civil War
- Wrote the song – When Johnny Comes Marching Home Again
- Twelve cannons, forty church bells, one thousand musicians, and ten thousand singers – during a five-day music festival
- Spirited illustrations with many sound words

Robertson, Sebastian. *Rock & Roll Highway: The Robbie Robertson Story.* (2014)
- Adam Gustavson, illustrator
- Biography - named one of the 100 best guitarists of all time by Rolling Stones
- Written by his son
- Taught to play guitar at 9 years old on a Native American reservation
- Was the lead guitarist for the rock group The Band
- Rich, nostalgia-tinged oil illustrations

Snicket, Lemony. *The Composer is Dead.* (2009)
- Carson Ellis, illustrator
- Murder mystery
- Wordplay, humor, and mild suspense
- Personification of the sections of the orchestra
- Good for young adults
- The watercolor illustrations combine caricatures of action with silhouettes of instruments

Hood, Susan. *Ada's Violin: The Story of the Recycled Orchestra of Paraguay.* (2016)
- Sally Wern Comport, illustrator
- True story of children in Paraguay, living on a landfill, making instruments from recycled trash

- A message of hope and innovation
- Acrylics and drawing illustrations

A monthly update, with many reviewed, additional titles, will be available to you if you email me at brainfitness78@gmail.com Log on to www.cognitive-fitness.com to see my other work.

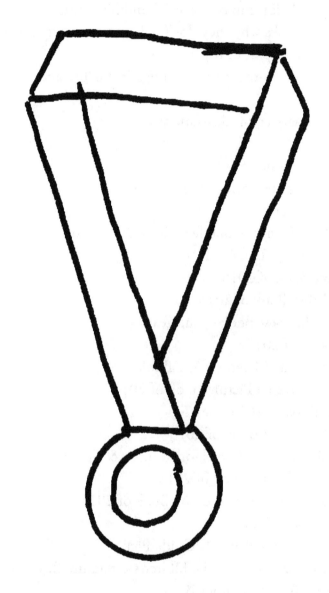

Character

CHARACTER

de la Peña, Matt. *Last Stop on Market Street.* (2015)
- Christian Robinson, illustrator
- About diversity and social engagement
- There is a wonderful relationship between CJ and his grandma
- As they ride the bus CJ asks why they don't have a car, why he doesn't have an iPad, and why do they get off in the dirty part of town
- His grandma helps him see the positive things in his life and the beauty around them and makes their ride fun
- Bold and cheerful primary color illustrations
- 2016 Newbery Medal
- 2016 Caldecott Honor Book
- 2016 Coretta Scott King Illustrator Honor Book
- New York Times Bestseller
- New York Times Book Review Notable Children's Book of 2015
- National Public Radio Best Book of 2015
- Kirkus Reviews Best Book of 2015
- Wall Street Journal Best Book of 2015
- 2015 Publishers Weekly Best Book of the Year
- Horn Book Best Book of 2015
- BookPage's 2015 First Must-Read Picture Book
- Huffington Post Best Overall Picture Book of 2015
- Boston Globe Best Book of 2015
- Chicago Public Library Best Book of 2015
- New York Public Library's 100 Books for Reading & Sharing
- Miami Herald Best Children's Book of 2015
- Raleigh News & Observer Best Children's Book of 2015
- Atlanta Parent Best Book of 2015
- San Francisco Chronicle Holiday Gift Guide Pick
- Center for the Study of Multicultural Children's Literature Best Multicultural Books of 2015
- Scholastic Instructor 50 Best Summer Books
- Association for Library Service to Children 2015 Summer Reading List
- Horn Book Summer 2015 Reading List
- School Library Journal's 2015 Top 10 Latin Books List
- Kansas City Star Thanksgiving 2015 Roundup Pick
- Winter 2014-2015 Kids' Indie Next Pick
- 2015 E.B. White Read Aloud Award Finalist
- 2016 Washington Children's Choice Picture Book Award
- 2016 Kentucky Bluegrass Award

CHARACTER

Graham, Bob. *How to Heal a Broken Wing*. (2008)
- A boy finds a fallen bird, takes it home and nurses it back to health
- Full-page illustrations, vertical and horizontal strips, and cartoon-style boxes in cloudy hues
- Empathy, problem-solving, kindness

Tan, Shaun. *The Lost Thing*. (2004)
- A boy is searching for treasures on the beach when he finds something he can't identify – so he brings it home
- An important commentary on seeing things differently
- Collage illustrations

Bunting, Eve. *Pop's Bridge*. (2006)
- C. F. Payne, illustrator
- Robert's father is a "high iron" worker or skywalker on the crew building the Golden Gate Bridge
- His friend Charlie's father, is a painter and Robert thinks that job is not as important
- Then scaffolding fails and workers fall to their deaths
- Mixed media illustrations

Girdner, Linda and Sarah Langford. *Grandfather's Story Cloth*. (2009)
- Stuart Loughridge, illustrator
- Chersheng's grandfather has Alzheimer's disease
- Grandfather had made a story cloth about his life in Laos and it now helps him to remember
- Chersheng creates a collage to help his grandfather remember his life in America
- The story is written in both English and Hmong
- Watercolor illustrations

Boelts, Maribeth. *Those Shoes*. (2009)
- Norah Z. Jones, illustrator
- A kids' view of the importance of the latest style of shoes in school
- Peer pressure, acceptance, and what is really important play a part in the story
- Colorful, full-page illustrations

Reynolds, Peter H. *Say Something*. (2019)
- Important message – if you see something – say something – an injustice? A brilliant idea?
- Our voices and our actions can speak volumes
- Speech bubbles with colorful backgrounds
- New York Times Bestseller

Agee, Jon. *The Wall in the Middle of the Book.* (2018)
- A foolish knight proclaims that his side of the wall is the safest side
- When he finds out he is in trouble on his side – those he least expects come to his rescue
- Thought-provoking tale about wall-building
- Colorful illustrations

Cali, Davide. *Queen of the Frogs.* (2017)
- Marco Soma, illustrator
- A story about leadership and the importance of humility
- A frog finds a crown at the bottom of the pool and proclaims herself queen
- She then expects the other frogs to serve her and entertain her
- Line drawings and shades of green illustrations

Hall, Michael. *Red: A Crayon's Story.* (2015)
- A story about the difficulties faced by a blue crayon in a red wrapper
- Everyone tries to help him be red but he is miserable
- About finding the courage to be true to your inner self
- Boldly colored and sharply detailed illustrations

Lanthier, Jennifer. *The Stamp Collector.* (2015)
- Francois Thisdale, illustrator
- A city boy who loves collecting postage stamps grows up to become a prison guard
- He befriends a prisoner who get letters with stamps from all over the world
- Illustrations with textured backgrounds and collages of postmarks from all over the world
- International Board on Books for Young People Honor List 2014
- 2017 Storytelling World Resource Awards honor in the Stories for Adolescent Listeners category
- 2013 Ezra Jack Keats New Writer Award Honor Book
- 2013 Amelia Frances Howard-Gibbon Illustrator's Award nominee
- Forest of Reading's Golden Oak 2014 winner
- 2014 Silver Birch Express Award nominee
- Ontario Library Association 2012 Best Bet - Picture Books category

Polacco, Patricia. *Junkyard Wonders.* (2010)
- Based on true events, Trisha finds out that at her new school her class is called the junkyard
- Her amazing teacher, however, does not allow her students to feel like misfits
- They visit a junkyard, find and refurbish a model plane, which they fly during the school's science fair
- Pencil and marker illustrations

Muth, Jon J. *Zen Shorts*. (2005)
- Stillwater the bear presents three short Buddhist tales told by three contemporary children
- Stillwater's questions are thought-provoking
- Lush watercolor illustrations
- Caldecott Honor Book

Polacco, Patricia. *Bully*. (2012)
- A story about online bullying – new 6th grade girls are friends and one is invited into the "celebrity" circle only to discover the group is humiliating her friend
- She leaves the group but then must endure the mean revenge of the celebrity group
- Good discussion starter for the middle school social scene
- Line and watercolor illustrations

John, Jory. *The Bad Seed*. (2017)
- Pete Oswald, illustrator
- The story of a sunflower seed gone bad
- Great discussion starter for how we treat others who are different
- Watercolor and digital paint illustrations
- New York Times Bestseller
- Amazon Best Children's Book of the Year

Reynolds, Peter. *The North Star*. (2009)
- Encouragement to follow the road less traveled – or to follow your dreams
- Charming ink and watercolor illustrations

Muth, Jon J. *The Three Questions: Based on a Story by Leo Tolstoy*. (2002)
- A boy, who in doing good deeds for others, finds inner peace
- A story about compassion and living in the moment
- Watercolor illustrations

Grimes, Nikki. *Thanks a Million*. (2006)
- Cozbi A. Cabrera, illustrator
- A story about gratitude and thankfulness
- Poetic verse – haiku, rebus, riddle
- Colorful illustrations

Thompson, Laurie Ann. *Emmanuel's Dream: The True Story of Emmanuel Ofosu Yeboah*. (2015)
- Sean Qualls, illustrator
- Story of a young man born in Ghana with a deformed leg
- He rode his bike four hundred miles across Ghana in 2001

- Message: disability is not inability
- Bold collage illustrations
- American Library Association Youth Media Awards Schneider Family Children's Book Award
- Association for Library Service to Children Notable Children's Book for 2016
- Cooperative Children's Book Center - Choices 2016
- 2015 Eureka Honor Award from the California Reading Association
- 2015 Cybils Award for Elementary/Middle Grade Non-Fiction
- 2016-2017 Georgia Children's Picturebook (Gr. K-4) Award
- Junior Library Guild
- FirstBook #StoriesForAll featured title
- Winter 2014-2015 Kids' Indie Next List
- Amazon Editors' Best Books of the Month Pick for January

Munson, Derek. *Enemy Pie*. (2000)
- Tara Calahan King, illustrator
- One little boy learns an effective recipe for turning a best enemy into a best friend
- Kindness, courtesy, respect, and friendship
- Getting along with difficult people
- Charming illustrations

Spires, Ashley. *The Most Magnificent Thing*. (2014)
- A starting point for future female engineers
- Emotions, solving problems
- Pen and ink and watercolor illustrations

Williams, Vera. *A Chair for My Mother*. (2007 reprint edition)
- After a fire destroys their home/possessions – a small family saves and saves to buy a comfortable chair
- Empathy, responsible decision-making
- Rich, vibrant colors – full-page illustrations
- Caldecott Honor Book

Woodson, Jacqueline. *Each Kindness*. (2012)
- E.B. Lewis, illustrator
- A new girl is rejected by the neighborhood girls and eventually stops trying
- Teacher shares how kindness can change the world – that hits home with the ones who were mean
- Watercolor illustrations
- Coretta Scott King Honor Award
- Jane Addams Peace Award

HOMELESSNESS

Williams, Laura E. *The Can Man.* (2017)
- Craig Orback, illustrator
- Money is tight and Tim realizes he won't be getting a skateboard for his birthday
- He hears the can man collecting empty soda cans and decides he will, too, and earn the money for the skateboard
- Then he meets the can man and realizes his plight and has a change of heart
- Full page oil illustrations

Sturgis, Brenda Reeves. *Still a Family: A Story About Homelessness.* (2017)
- Jo-Shin Lee, illustrator
- A little girl tells the story of the family's homelessness – living in a shelter – with her mom in one while her dad is in a separate shelter for men
- She describes eating at a soup kitchen and wearing shoes that don't fit
- But she also tells of meeting her dad in the park and playing and enjoying each other's company
- Crayon and watercolor illustrations

Bunting, Eve. *Fly Away Home.* (1993)
- Ronald Himler, illustrator
- A homeless boy and his father live in an airport moving from terminal to terminal so as not to be discovered
- When a trapped bird finally finds freedom – the boy and his father have hope for the future
- Watercolor illustrations

Polacco, Patricia. *I Can Hear the Sun.* (1999)
- A modern myth created by the author
- A young boy helps a neighbor girl care for a flock of geese
- When the geese prepare to fly south for the winter – the boy says he is going also
- Brown, peach, and green illustrations

McGovern. Ann. *The Lady in the Box.* (1997)
- Marni Backer, illustrator
- A story about homelessness
- A young boy and his sister help a lady who lives in a box over a heating vent outside of a delicatessen
- Soft-toned illustrations

A monthly update, with many reviewed, additional titles, will be available to you if you email me at brainfitness78@gmail.com Log on to www.cognitive-fitness.com to see my other work.

Miscellaneous

MISCELLANEOUS

Hopkinson, Deborah. *Sky Boys: How They Built the Empire State Building.* (2012)
- James Ransome, illustrator
- It took hundreds of men leveling, shoveling, hauling, and hoisting 60,000 tons of steel, and stacking 10 million bricks
- The story told by father and son who worked on the build and were among the first to the top when the completed building opened
- Stunning oil illustrations
- Boston Globe–Horn Book Honor Book
- American Library Association/Association for Library Service to Children Notable Children's Book

Gerstein, Mordicai. *The Man Who Walked Between the Towers.* (2007)
- The story of a daring tightrope walk between skyscrapers
- In 1974, French aerialist Philippe Petit - between the two towers of the World Trade Center
- Excellent illustrations showing breath-taking perspectives
- 2004 Caldecott Medal
- 2004 Boston Globe - Horn Book Award for Picture Books
- 2006 Carnegie Medal for Excellence in Children's Video.

Polacco, Patricia. *John Phillip Duck.* (2005)
- The story of the Peabody Hotel Marching Ducks
- Every morning at 11 o'clock a group of ducks exits an elevator and enters the lobby of the Peabody Hotel in Memphis, TN
- They parade on a red carpet to a fountain in step to a John Philip Sousa march, led by a uniformed Duckmaster
- They swim there all day and then return to their rooftop home
- This happens at the Peabody Hotel in Orlando, FL, as well
- Beautiful illustrations

Rocco, John. *Black Out.* (2011)
- Reminiscent of the New York City 2003 black out
- A family is cooking dinner, watching TV, and on the computer when the lights go out in the entire city
- On the roof top they escape the heat and end up having a block party in the sky with their neighbors
- When it is over the family decides it wasn't so bad and really great to take a break
- Full-page illustrations that go from full color to back-and-white
- 2012 Caldecott Honor Book

- New York Times Notable Book
- Wall Street Journal Best Book of the Year
- Publisher's Weekly Best Book of the Year
- School Library Journal Best Book of the Year
- Kirkus Reviews Best Book of the Year

Sorell, Traci. *We Are Grateful: Otsaliheliga.* (2018)
- Frane Lessac, illustrator
- Story told by an enrolled citizen of the Cherokee Nation
- The story of Native American life described through celebrations and experiences over a full year
- The word "otsaliheliga" is used to express gratitude
- Colorful, folk art-style illustrations
- 2019 Sibert Honor Book
- 2019 Orbis Pictus Honor Book
- National Public Radio Guide to 2018's Great Reads
- 2018 Book Launch Award - Society of Children's Book Writers and Illustrators
- Kirkus Reviews Best Books of 2018
- School Library Journal Best Books of 2018
- 2018 Junior Library Guild selection
- 2019 Reading the West Picture Book Award

Goldstyn, Jacques. *Letters to A Prisoner.* (2017) WORDLESS
- Angela Keenlyside, illustrator
- Inspired by Amnesty International's letter-writing campaign to help free the people who have been imprisoned for voicing their opinions
- Watercolor, ink, and colored pencil illustrations on a white background

Fleischman, Paul. *Westlandia.* (2002)
- Kevin Hawkes, illustrator
- A young nonconformist invents a self-sufficient civilization in his suburban backyard
- Wesley develops a whole civilization from the garden he plants in his backyard
- Colorful and comical illustrations

Lin, Grace. *A Big Mooncake for Little Star.* (2018)
- An origin story of the phases of the moon
- Vibrant gouache illustrations
- Caldecott Honor Book
- Horn Book Fanfare 2018

- Chicago Public Library Best Book 0f 2018
- Shelf Awareness Best Book of 2018
- Center for the Study of Multicultural Children's Literature Best Book of 2018
- Boston Globe Best Book of 2018
- 2018 Nerdies List Book
- American Library Association 2019 Children's Notables List

Woodson, Jacqueline. *The Day You Begin*. (2018)
- Rafael Lopez, illustrator
- A great story for starting a new school or job or activity
- We all feel like outsiders sometimes - and how brave it is that we move on anyway
- Sometimes - when we reach out and begin to share our stories, others will be happy to meet us halfway
- Collaged patterns and textures in full page illustrations

Lê, Mihn. *Drawn Together*. (2018)
- Dan Santat, illustrator
- Almost wordless picture book
- A young boy tries to communicate with his non-English speaking grandfather
- They eventually are able to communicate by drawing pictures
- Luminous illustrations
- Asian/Pacific American Award for Literature

Myers, Walter Dean. *Looking Like Me*. (2009)
- Christopher Myers, illustrator
- Poetic celebration with vibrant illustrations highlighting the uniqueness of each individual
- Illustrations – collage and photographs – useful for art class

Weitzman, Jacqueline Preiss. *You Can't Take a Balloon into the National Gallery*. (2000) WORDLESS
- Robin Glasser, illustrator
- Story of two children and their grandmother and their visit to the National Gallery
- At the same time the girl's balloon escapes and does parallel visits to famous places around D. C.
- Pen and ink and watercolor illustrations

Cooper, Melrose. *Gettin' Through Thursday*. (1998)
- Nneka Bennett, illustrator
- Thursday is a bad day for Andre - it is the day before Mama gets paid and things are always tight
- He is going to make the honor roll on Thursday and has been promised a party – how?
- Watercolor and colored pencil illustrations

MISCELLANEOUS

Woodson, Jacqueline. *Our Gracie Aunt.* (2002)
- Jon J. Muth, illustrator
- Beebee and Johnson's mother has not come home for several days
- A social worker takes them to live with their aunt who provides a warm and caring home
- They hope someday their mother will be able to care for them again
- Subtle watercolor illustrations

Snicket, Lemony. *The Dark.* (2013)
- Jon Klassen, illustrator
- Lazlo is afraid of the dark which usually lives in the basement
- Gouache and digital illustrations
- Bulletin of the Center for Children's Books Blue Ribbon Picture Book Award

Petty, Dev. *I Don't Want to Be a Frog.* (2018)
- Mike Boldt, illustrator
- The hero wants to be anything but a slimy frog
- Then when the hungry wolf arrives – he changes his mind
- Richly colored comic illustrations

Tregonning, Mel. *Small Things.* (2018) WORDLESS
- About childhood anxiety
- Incredibly moving tale
- Pencil illustrations
- 2018 Foreword Independent Booksellers Award: Graphic Novels & Comics Bronze
- 2019 United States Board on Books for Young People Outstanding International Books – Grades 6-8
- 2019 Pop Culture Classroom Excellence in Graphic Literature Awards: Best in Children's Graphic Literature
- 2018 *Horn Book* "August 2018 Back-to-School Horn Book Herald: Intermediate"
- 2018 National Council for Teachers of English "Spring into New Book Recommendations"
- 2018 *School Library Journal* blogger Elizabeth Bird's "2018 Books with a Message"
- 2018 *School Library Journal* blogger Elizabeth Bird's "2018 Wordless Picture Books"
- 2018 *The Children's Book Review* "The Best Kids Chapter Books and Novels of 2018"
- 2018 *The Children's Book Review* "Best New Books for Tweens & PreTeens | March 2018"
- 2017 Gold Ledger Award (Australia)
- 2017 Australian Book Design Awards - Best Designed Children's Illustrated Book (Australia)
- 2017 Children's Book Council of Australia Book of the Year, Crichton Award for New Illustrators (Australia)
- 2017 Children's Book Council of Australia Picture Book of the Year (Australia)

Markel, Michelle. *Balderdash!: John Newbery and the Boisterous Birth of Children's Books.* (2017)
- Nancy Carpenter, illustrator
- Biography of John Newbery
- He was a well-loved author and printer
- Sepia ink illustrations - pages are digitally made to look old and weathered

A monthly update, with many reviewed, additional titles, will be available to you if you email me at brainfitness78@gmail.com Log on to www.cognitive-fitness.com to see my other work.

Liz Knowles, Ed.D.

With 12 published books and extensive experience both as a teacher and administrator in the field of education, Liz Knowles, Ed.D. has been making a profound impact on the lives of countless teachers, parents, and children throughout her distinguished career.

After earning her undergraduate degree in Elementary Education from Central Connecticut State University, Dr. Knowles began her career as an elementary school teacher, eventually landing at Pine Crest School (then Boca Raton Academy) in South Florida in 1980. She taught fourth and sixth grade while earning her master's in Reading and her doctorate in Curriculum Development and Systemic Change from Nova Southeastern University. As a result, Dr. Knowles was appointed Director of Professional Development and Curriculum at Pine Crest in 1996.

At Pine Crest, Dr. Knowles assisted more than 300 faculty members on two campuses with curriculum mapping and implementation, provided a comprehensive teaching certification program, developed and taught in-service classes, served as a consultant to faculty, and outlined a school improvement plan while shepherding several accreditation processes.

In addition, she was an adjunct professor in the Graduate Teacher Education Program at Nova Southeastern University and taught graduate-level courses at Florida Atlantic University. Beginning in 1997, she completed the first of her 12 books, *The Reading Connection: Bringing Parents, Teachers, and Librarians Together*. This text, like her subsequent publications, serves parents and educational professionals by offering tips and titles aimed at promoting children's literacy.

Always seeking a new challenge, Dr. Knowles left Pine Crest in 2009 after 29 years of faithful service. She next served as Director of Content (K-12) for Kaplan Virtual Education. An engaging speaker, Dr. Knowles has made several presentations at conferences throughout the country on various educational topics. She is also the recipient of the International Reading Association Middle School Special Interest Group Literacy Award and was the Anti-Defamation League's 2009 honoree at the Eighth Annual Palm Beach Educator Awards Luncheon.

Dr. Knowles also served as Head of Studies, Director of Professional Development, and Diploma Program Coordinator at Boca Prep International School an International Baccalaureate School in Boca Raton. She also spent several years writing curriculum and applications for charter schools in Palm Beach County.

Dr. Knowles has always been interested in the latest educational research and in sharing her findings and recommendations with colleagues and parents. A special interest has always been current brain research and how it can be utilized most effectively in the classroom. For two years she was owner/director of a brain training center in Boca Raton and now, through Cognitive Advantage, LLC and www.cognitive-fitness.com. Dr. Knowles teaches classes, small groups and private lessons on brain fitness. She sells a program, complete with materials and a book, "DIY Cognitive Fitness" to assisted living and clubhouse communities as well as to schools.

She lived in Nassau, Bahamas and traveled the Caribbean, she lived in Milan, Italy for almost a year and traveled Europe. She has spent a week in China and recently she has been to Donegal, Ireland, Barcelona, Spain, and Cairo, Luxor, and Aswan, Egypt.

A monthly update, with many reviewed, additional titles, will be available to you if you email me at brainfitness78@gmail.com Log on to www.cognitive-fitness.com to see my other work.

CPSIA information can be obtained
at www.ICGtesting.com
Printed in the USA
BVHW010726301121
622796BV00010B/64